Editor

Erica N. Russikoff, M.A.

Editor in Chief

Karen J. Goldfluss, M.S. Ed.

Creative Director

Sarah M. Fournier

Cover Artist

Barb Lorseyedi

Illustrator

Kelly McMahon

Art Coordinator

Renée Mc Elwee

Imaging

Craig Gunnell

Publisher

Mary D. Smith, M.S. Ed.

Grade 2

Teacher Created Resources
TCR 3892

Nonfiction
PAIRED

D0940034

NONFICTION

FICTION

- Contains fiction and nonfiction passages on a variety of topics
- Includes critical-thinking questions to improve comprehension
- Extends the reading by using interactive writing activities
- Correlated to the Common Core State Standards

Teacher Created Resources

This is a tapsponder enabled resource! See inside book cover for details.

Author

Susan Mackey Collins, M. Ed.

CORRELATED TO **COMMON CORE** STANDARDS

For correlations to the Common Core State Standards, see pages 143–144. Correlations can also be found at *http://www.teachercreated.com/standards*.

Teacher Created Resources

6421 Industry Way
Westminster, CA 92683
www.teachercreated.com

ISBN: 978-1-4206-3892-9

© *2015 Teacher Created Resources*
Made in U.S.A.

Teacher Created Resources

Table of Contents

Table of Contents (cont.)

Introduction

Making connections is an important part of everyday life. People strive daily to make connections with other people, events, and experiences. Making connections plays an important role in nearly everything one does. It is not surprising then that this skill must also be used in developing great readers.

Connections are vital in developing fluency in reading and in understanding a variety of texts. *Nonfiction & Fiction Paired Texts* helps emergent readers learn to make connections with both fiction and nonfiction texts. The activities in this book also help fluent readers to enhance and increase their developing reading skills. *Nonfiction & Fiction Paired Texts* is the perfect reading tool for all levels of readers.

The high-interest texts in *Nonfiction & Fiction Paired Texts* contain both fiction and nonfiction passages. The units are written in pairs that share a common idea or theme. The first passage in each unit is fiction. A nonfiction text follows each fiction story. Subjects in each unit are varied, providing a multitude of topics to engage the various interests of the readers. Topics are also age-appropriate and will appeal to children in the corresponding grade level. While reading the texts, students are encouraged to look for specific meanings and to make logical inferences from what is read.

Each unit in *Nonfiction & Fiction Paired Texts* has five pages. The texts in each set are followed by two assessment pages that contain multiple-choice questions and short-answer writing activities. These pages are designed to meet the rigor demanded by the Common Core State Standards. Each assessment leads students to look for and generally cite textual evidence when answering questions. A third page in the assessment section of each unit includes longer writing activities. The writing activities for each unit are tied to higher-order thinking and questioning skills. The writing ideas are designed to help assess a student's ability to respond to a written prompt while incorporating the skills of excellent writing.

Nonfiction & Fiction Paired Texts was written to help students gain important reading skills and practice responding to questions based on the Common Core State Standards. The different units provide practice with a multitude of standards and skills, including but not limited to the following:

- making and understanding connections between content-rich reading materials

- building reading-comprehension skills

- analyzing, comparing, and contrasting fiction and nonfiction texts

- sequencing and summarizing

- experience with text-based, multiple-choice questions

- practice with short-answer responses

- practice in developing written responses to various prompts

- understanding the genres of fiction and nonfiction texts

- quoting from texts to complete assessments

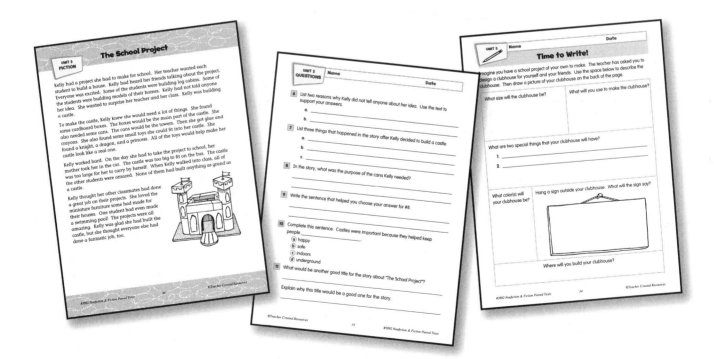

How to Use This Book

Nonfiction & Fiction Paired Texts is divided into twenty-six units. Each unit has five pages. The first two pages are texts that share a common topic or theme. Each unit contains both a fiction and nonfiction selection, as well as three assessment pages.

The book is designed so that each unit can be used separately. The activities can be completed in order, starting with the first unit and working through unit twenty-six, or they can be completed in random order. Anyone using the book may want to look for common themes or ideas that correspond with other units being taught in other subject areas. The units in this book can be used to help teach across the curriculum and to easily tie in reading and writing skills to other areas of study.

Provided with each set of fiction and nonfiction stories are three pages of assessment activities. Two of the three pages are multiple-choice and short-answer questions, which rely heavily on text-based answers. The last page in each unit is a writing page. The teacher may choose to use all three pages after completion of the connected texts, or he or she may choose to only use specific pages for assessment. Pages can be done during regular academic hours or be sent home for extra practice. Students may work on assignments alone or work with partners or in small groups.

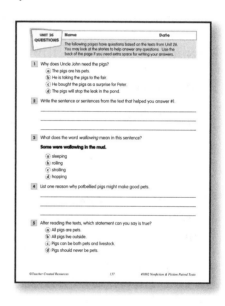

Looking at the answer key, one will notice that not all questions have answers. Many questions require short answers, which can vary, as long as the answers are based on the text. The Common Core State Standards require students to support their answer choices with information from texts, not personal opinions. Completion of the short-answer questions gives students the opportunity to practice writing their answers using information from what they have read in each unit. Of course, creativity is an equally important learning tool and is not ignored in these units. Students are given opportunities to express their own ideas and thoughts, especially in the Time to Write! activities. The writing activities are tied to the texts but are geared to give students the chance to practice the skills needed to be successful writers.

In grading the short-answer questions, teachers must verify that the answers are included in the text. Assessing the responses in the Time to Write! section is up to the teacher's discretion. Each teacher knows the abilities of the individual students in his or her class. Answers provided at one point in the year may be considered satisfactory; however, as the year progresses, the teacher's expectations of the student's writing skills will have greatly increased. A student would eventually be expected to provide better-developed responses and written work with fewer mistakes. A good idea is to keep a folder with samples of the student's work from different times during the academic year. Teachers, parents, and students can easily see progress made with the skills necessary for good writing by comparing samples from earlier in the year to the student's present writing samples.

The units in *Nonfiction & Fiction Paired Texts* can also be used to help students understand the basic principles of text. One way to do this is to teach students to use a specific reading method. Students can use the UNC method (see pages 8–9) to help gain a better understanding of how text is presented on the page and to develop and refine skills for reading for detail. After the UNC method is mastered, students will learn to automatically employ these skills in their everyday reading without having to be coached to complete the process. The skills of good reading will become automatic.

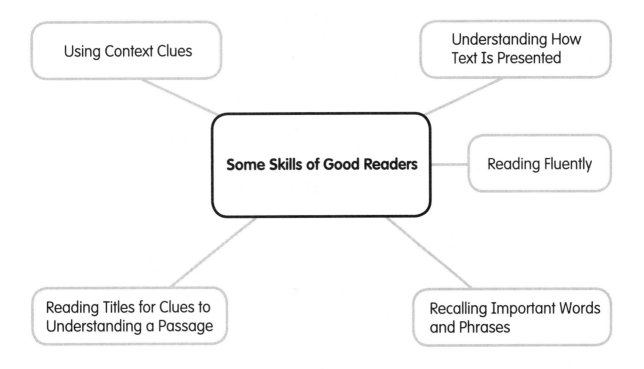

Using Context Clues

Understanding How Text Is Presented

Some Skills of Good Readers

Reading Fluently

Reading Titles for Clues to Understanding a Passage

Recalling Important Words and Phrases

Understanding and Using the UNC Method

U <u>Underline</u> and read all titles.

N Place <u>numbers</u> by all the paragraphs.

C Put <u>circles</u> around or highlight all important words and phrases in the text.

When students are presented with a text, they can use the UNC method to help break down the material. Students immediately underline and read all titles. To better manage the material, students next add a number beside each paragraph. This helps teachers as they go over questions. They can easily ask the students to look at a specific paragraph to point out information that helped to answer a particular question. Using this method, teachers may also discover there are students who have simply not learned how to tell where a paragraph begins or ends. This explains why many times when a teacher asks a student to read a specific paragraph, he or she cannot. The student may honestly be unsure of where to start!

The final step in the UNC method is to circle or highlight important words or phrases in the text. By completing this step, students are required to read for detail. At first, the teacher may find that many students will want to highlight entire paragraphs. Teachers will want to use a sample unit to guide students through the third step. Teachers can make copies of a unit already highlighted to help show students how to complete the third step. Teachers can work through a unit together with the students, or they may even want to use a document camera so the students can easily see the process as they work on a unit together in class. Students will soon discover that there are important details and context clues that can be used to help understand which information is the most important in any given text.

Students need to have confidence in their abilities to succeed at any given task. This is where the UNC method is a bonus in any classroom. When using this method, students can be successful in reading any text and answering the questions that follow.

The UNC method is especially helpful in aiding students to carefully read new or unfamiliar texts. Highlighters are helpful when working with printed texts but are not necessary. (For example, students can use different highlighter colors to complete each step.) Students who consistently use this method will eventually no longer need to physically highlight or circle the text as the necessary skills to great reading become an automatic response with any text. Students who consistently practice the UNC method make mental maps of what they have read and often no longer need to look back at the text when answering the questions! The UNC method allows students who are kinesthetic learners to have a physical activity that can take place during a reading activity. Visual learners are greatly aided by this method, as well. Students are encouraged by their positive progress and look forward to the challenge of reading a new text.

UNIT 7
FICTION

Dinosaurs Roar

(1) Joey and Josh were happy to be visiting their uncle. The twins loved going to work with their Uncle Rick. Uncle Rick worked with a company that helped make movies. This time, the movie was all about dinosaurs. Uncle Rick told Joey and Josh that they were about to see some amazing things.

(2) "Follow me, boys," Uncle Rick said to Joey and Josh. Joey and Josh walked through the door. They could not believe what they were seeing. In a large room on the other side of the door were dinosaurs. They were everywhere!

(3) "Wow!" Joey said. "These dinosaurs look so real!"

(4) "Did you help make these?" Josh asked his uncle.

(5) Uncle Rick nodded. "Yes. These dinosaurs are part of a new movie. They need to look very real for the movie we are making. I am glad you both think they look like real dinosaurs."

(6) Joey and Josh walked around and looked at the huge creatures up close. There was a Tyrannosaurus rex, a Stegosaurus, and even a Triceratops!

(7) All of a sudden, the dinosaurs started to move. Joey and Josh both screamed and started to run, but there was no place to go. They were surrounded by moving dinosaurs. There was no sign of their uncle, but then they saw him. He was smiling. He didn't look scared at all.

(8) "Relax, boys. I was just playing a joke. The dinosaurs are not alive. They are animatronics. They work like a remote-control car would. I can make them move and even roar. Would you two like to try?"

(9) Uncle Rick was not surprised when both boys said yes!

#3892 Nonfiction & Fiction Paired Texts   40   *©Teacher Created Resources*

What's in the Box?

Mac wanted a pet. His mom said she was bringing him a surprise home from work. Mac hoped the surprise was a pet. He wanted a furry pet that could cuddle up next to him. He had tried to prove to his parents he could take care of an animal. He had been keeping his room clean and doing extra chores at home.

Mac heard his mom's car pull into the driveway. He opened the door to run and see what she had for him. Mac could hardly wait to see his surprise.

"Hello, Mac," his mother said as she hugged him.

"Did you bring me a surprise?" Mac asked her.

Mac's mother laughed. She knew Mac was too excited to even tell her hello. She walked to the back of the car and opened the door. Mac watched as she lifted out a brown box. Mac could not wait to see what was inside.

"Follow me into the house," his mother said. Mac ran ahead of her and opened the front door. He hurried over as his mother put the box on the ground. When he looked inside, he could not believe what was in the box! Two kittens were curled up against each other. The kittens looked up at Mac, and both began to purr. Mac scooped up the kittens. He tucked one under his left arm. He tucked the other one under his right arm.

"Mom, I was hoping for one pet. I am so happy you got me two pets!"

Mac's mother explained that the two kittens were sisters. She did not want them to be apart from each other. She knew Mac would take good care of them. He had shown her over the last few days just how responsible he could be.

Mac looked at the kittens and then at his mother. He knew in his heart that he would not let any of them down.

The Perfect Pet?

In 1975, a man named Gary Dahl came up with the perfect pet. One night, he was talking with his friends. Gary and his friends talked about how most pets were fun, but they were also a lot of work. Gary had an idea. He knew what would make the perfect pet. He began telling everyone that a rock would be the best pet of all.

Gary's idea of a rock as a pet was a joke, but people wanted to buy Gary's pet rocks. He put each pet rock in a box. The box even had air holes. Next, each pet rock got its own nest. The nest helped keep the pet rock warm and safe.

The rocks Gary sold as pets could be found in stores. People loved buying the pets. People thought the idea was funny. One thing that was very funny was the book that came with each pet. The book told how to take care of the rock. The book also explained how to teach the rock how to do tricks. Everyone who owned a pet rock found out that teaching a pet rock to stay was a very easy trick.

Gary Dahl's pet rocks are not as popular anymore. Most people don't even think about getting a rock as a pet today. But, if you want the perfect pet, maybe you could adopt a rock of your own. If you do, be sure to teach your rock to sit and stay the minute you get your new pet. Then you really can have the perfect pet.

The following pages have questions based on the texts from Unit 1. You may look at the stories to help answer any questions. Use the back of the page if you need extra space for writing your answers.

1 How are both stories the same?

   (a) They both tell how hard it is to have a pet.

   (b) They both tell that kittens are the best pets.

   (c) They are both about someone who loves dogs.

   (d) They are both about pets.

2 How might Mac have felt if he had been given a pet rock?

   (a) He would have been disappointed.

   (b) He would have been glad.

   (c) He would have been afraid.

   (d) He would have been embarrassed.

Explain why you chose your answer for #2. _____

_____

_____

3 Which **two** answers are most likely true about both stories?

   (a) There is no such thing as a perfect pet.

   (b) Kittens are the only perfect pets.

   (c) Taking care of a real pet is a lot of work.

   (d) Anyone can adopt a dog.

4 Which sentence from the fiction story best shows that Mac likes his new pets?

   (a) When he looked inside, he could not believe what was in the box!

   (b) Mac scooped up the kittens.

   (c) "Mom, I was hoping for one pet."

   (d) "I am so happy you got me two pets!"

5 Why do you think the story title "The Perfect Pet?" has a question mark at the end of the title?

_____

_____

6 Mac thinks a kitten is the perfect pet. List two reasons why Mac would think a kitten is a better pet than a rock.

a. _____

_____

b. _____

_____

7 List in order three things that happened in the story "What's in the Box?"

a. _____

_____

b. _____

_____

c. _____

_____

8 Write one adjective to describe each pet.

Pet	Adjective
a. kitten	_____
b. rock	_____

9 Complete this sentence: Pet rocks were successful because people thought they were _____.

ⓐ scary   ⓒ angry
ⓑ funny   ⓓ nice

10 Write the sentence from the story that helped you answer #9.

_____

_____

Time to Write!

Imagine you want there to be no more pets in the world. Explain your reasons. Tell why people should no longer have pets. Be sure to write three reasons why people shouldn't have pets. (Example: Pets get fur all over the house.)

Reason 1

Reason 2

Reason 3

Something Extra: On the back of the page, write three reasons why people really should have pets.

Counting Down the Days

Kim had been counting down the days until Saturday. She could not believe it was finally here. Her birthday was always great, but this year her parents were taking her to the circus. She had never been to the circus. She could not wait to go.

Last week, Kim had heard her mother telling her father the circus would be in town. When her parents had asked her what she wanted for her special day, she had said tickets to the circus. They had bought tickets for all three of them to go. Now her wish was about to come true.

The clown greeted Kim and her parents when they got out of the car. Kim laughed when she saw two clowns walking on stilts. They looked funny standing on two long poles. One clown was driving a tiny car. Another was running from a clown who carried a bucket of water. All of the clowns were outside the giant circus tent. Kim could only imagine what would be going on inside the tent with so much going on outside.

Kim's dad walked beside her as they entered the tent. He held her hand as they walked up the stairs and found seats in the stands. He paid a man for a necklace that glowed. She put the circle of light around her neck. She only had time to say "thank you" before the show began.

The lights dimmed, and a man's voice boomed over the speakers. Kim did not know what would happen next, but she didn't care. It was already the best birthday she could ever remember!

6   How can the reader tell Kim is enjoying the circus?

_____

_____

_____

_____

7   Based on the passage, what can the reader conclude Kim's feelings are about going to the circus?

_____

_____

_____

_____

8   What would be another good title for the story "Counting Down the Days"?

_____

9   Which passage gives the most factual information about clowns? Circle your choice.

fiction passage   **nonfiction passage**

10   Which sentence from one of the passages best explains your answer choice for #9?

_____

_____

_____

_____

Time to Write!

Imagine you are applying for a job as a clown at the circus. Write three reasons why the circus should give you the job.

1. _____

2. _____

3. _____

Draw and color a picture of you as a clown.

Write three sentences to describe your picture.

1. _____

2. _____

3. _____

Up in the Sky

Matt was glad to be at his grandparents' house. He loved spending the night with his grandmother and grandfather. Matt lived with his mother in the city. His grandparents lived on a farm. On the farm, he saw lots of animals, and he played outside each day. At night, his grandparents liked to take him outside and look at the stars. In the city, the lights were so bright that he could not see all the stars.

"Do you see that star?" Matt's grandfather asked him as he pointed straight up.

Matt looked where his grandfather was pointing. He loved the bright North Star. It was one of his favorites to look at.

"Yes, Grandfather," he answered. "That star is beautiful."

As the two looked up, a sudden flash went across the sky.

"What was that?" Matt's grandmother was the first to speak.

Neither Matt nor his grandfather answered her. They both just looked at each other. Finally, Matt spoke up.

"Did that look like a flying saucer to you?"

Grandpa smiled and then said, "Well, I have to agree with you. It did look like a UFO."

Then Matt's grandmother said, "Aren't you glad you came to stay at the farm, Matt? You got to see cows, chickens, horses, and a flying saucer."

Matt was filled with excitement. He knew he would never look at the night sky again without looking for UFOs.

What's in the Sky?

Look up at the sky. What do you see? Are there stars or clouds? Are there airplanes or birds? There are many things to see when you look up. Sometimes, when people look at the sky, they see things they are not sure about. They do not know what they are seeing. Many people call these unusual sights UFOs or "unidentified flying objects." Some people think UFOs are from other planets. People all over the world believe they have seen things in the sky that cannot be explained.

Some reports of strange things in the sky can be explained. Some countries have secret airships that are shaped like discs. In World War II, Germany made a disc-shaped aircraft. This flying saucer was very fast. Also, some clouds look like saucer shapes. The clouds are shaped in the form of a disc. The clouds have tricked many people into thinking they have seen flying saucers.

Whether you believe in aliens or not, it is always fun to look up at the sky and see what might be there. Maybe you can explain what you see . . . or maybe not!

UNIT 3 QUESTIONS

Name _____ **Date** _____

The following pages have questions based on the texts from Unit 3. You may look at the stories to help answer any questions. Use the back of the page if you need extra space for writing your answers.

1 Which event happened first in the story "Up in the Sky"?

(a) Matt and his grandparents saw something strange in the sky.

(b) Matt went to spend the night with his grandparents.

(c) Matt's grandfather showed him the North Star.

(d) Matt asked his grandparents if they had seen the same thing he did.

2 Choose the synonym or word that means the same as *unidentified* as it is used in this sentence:

Many people call these unusual sights UFOs or "unidentified flying objects."

(a) familiar

(b) same

(c) unknown

(d) large

3 According to the text, what does the letter "F" stand for in *UFO*?

_____

4 What is the same about both stories?

(a) Both have people looking at the sky.

(b) Both are about sightings of unidentified objects.

(c) Both are about people visiting farms.

(d) Both explain what UFOs are.

5 Why could Matt not see the stars as well in the city?

(a) There were no stars to see.

(b) He went to bed too early.

(c) The lights were too bright in the city.

(d) He never tried to look at the stars in the city.

6 Matt thinks he may have seen an alien ship in the sky. List two more things someone can see in the sky.

a. _____

b. _____

7 Use the text to help you explain why someone might think a cloud was a flying saucer.

_____

_____

_____

_____

_____

8 Write two words that would best describe Matt's trip to his grandparents' farm.

a. _____

b. _____

9 Write a word that is the opposite of one of the words you wrote in #8.

_____

10 Choose one of the words from #8. Then explain why you chose this word to describe Matt's trip to the farm.

_____

_____

_____

_____

_____

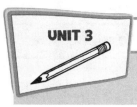

Time to Write!

Part 1

Imagine you have seen a UFO in the sky. Describe what you saw. Use the form below to help you write about the UFO. Write your answers in complete sentences.

What size was the UFO?	What color was the UFO?
What shape was the UFO?	Who might have built the UFO?

Part 2

Draw and color a picture of the UFO you described in Part 1.

Vacation Cruise

"We are going on a cruise for our summer vacation," Madison's parents told her at breakfast.

Madison smiled at the news. She had never been on a big ship before. She had ridden in a canoe at camp. Only two people fit in the canoe. A ship would hold much more than two people. She was nervous but excited.

"Where will we be going?" Madison asked.

Her mother put a pancake on Madison's plate. Then she answered her. "We are taking a cruise to Bermuda."

"Bermuda!" Madison exclaimed. "Does that mean we will have to go near the Bermuda Triangle?" Madison had watched a show about the mystery of the Bermuda Triangle. Things had been known to disappear in the area. She was not sure she wanted to cruise past such a strange place.

"Don't worry about the stories you have heard." Her dad smiled at her and took a bite of his pancake.

"Ships sail to Bermuda every day, Madison," her mother said. "Don't worry about that."

"There is one thing you should worry about," her dad said.

Both Madison and her mother looked at her father. She wondered what it could be.

"The only thing you need to worry about is if you have enough bathing suits for the big trip!"

6 The Bermuda Triangle is a strange place. List two strange things that happened there.

a. _____

_____

b. _____

_____

7 Where had Madison learned about the Bermuda Triangle?

_____

_____

8 Should Madison be afraid to go on the trip? Why or why not?

_____

_____

9 The Bermuda Triangle is a mysterious place. Which word is a synonym for *mysterious*?

ⓐ fancy

ⓑ fun

ⓒ slow

ⓓ strange

10 Madison said she had been on a canoe trip. She had never been on a big ship. Use information from the text to explain how the two trips are different.

_____

_____

_____

_____

_____

Time to Write!

Many people are scared to travel near the Bermuda Triangle. Imagine you own a hotel on an island. Anyone coming to your hotel must pass through the Bermuda Triangle. List three reasons why people should not be afraid to travel to your hotel.

1. _____

   _____

2. _____

   _____

3. _____

   _____

In the space below, draw a picture of your hotel. Write three words or phrases that best describe the picture.

1. _____

2. _____

3. _____

The School Project

Kelly had a project she had to make for school. Her teacher wanted each student to build a house. Kelly had heard her friends talking about the project. Everyone was excited. Some of the students were building log cabins. Some of the students were building models of their homes. Kelly had not told anyone her idea. She wanted to surprise her teacher and her class. Kelly was building a castle.

To make the castle, Kelly knew she would need a lot of things. She found some cardboard boxes. The boxes would be the main part of the castle. She also needed some cans. The cans would be the towers. Then she got glue and crayons. She also found some small toys she could fit into her castle. She found a knight, a dragon, and a princess. All of the toys would help make her castle look like a real one.

Kelly worked hard. On the day she had to take the project to school, her mother took her in the car. The castle was too big to fit on the bus. The castle was too large for her to carry by herself. When Kelly walked into class, all of the other students were amazed. None of them had built anything as grand as a castle.

Kelly thought her other classmates had done a great job on their projects. She loved the miniature furniture some had made for their houses. One student had even made a swimming pool! The projects were all amazing. Kelly was glad she had built the castle, but she thought everyone else had done a fantastic job, too.

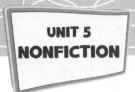
Castles

Castles were made to keep people who lived there safe. The castles were made to protect the people from other people who might want to hurt them. The outside was made of stone. This was to protect it from fire.

Outside the castle was a moat. A moat is a large ditch. The moat would go all the way around the castle. This ditch was sometimes filled with water. Sometimes, the moat was filled with stakes or sharp sticks. The main way to enter the castle would be across a bridge. This bridge could only be lowered by the people inside the castle. If the enemy tried to cross the moat, people inside the castle had more time to try to stop them.

Another important part of a castle is the towers. Towers were built along the walls of the castle. Archers could shoot their arrows from the towers. The towers helped protect them from anyone below. The towers also allowed the people inside the castle to see far below them.

Castles were made to help keep people safe, but many people today think they are beautiful to look at. A castle would have been a cold place to live. But the people inside would have known they were in a safe place.

UNIT 5 QUESTIONS

Name

Date

The following pages have questions based on the texts from Unit 5. You may look at the stories to help answer any questions. Use the back of the page if you need extra space for writing your answers.

1 Which phrase best describes a castle?

    (a) a small house made of logs

    (b) a large building made of stone

    (c) a shelter built underground

    (d) a pyramid built out of stones

2 Which sentence from the nonfiction text helped you to answer #1?

_____

_____

_____

_____

3 How did Kelly feel about her project?

    (a) She thought hers was good, but she liked the other students' projects, too.

    (b) She thought hers was better than the other students.

    (c) She did not like her project.

    (d) She did not finish her project.

4 Which sentence best explains why a moat was built around the castle?

    (a) Castles were made to keep those who lived there safe.

    (b) Outside the castle was a moat.

    (c) If the enemy tried to cross the moat, people inside the castle had more time to try to stop them.

    (d) A moat is a large ditch.

5 Write two words that would best describe Kelly.

    a. _____

    b. _____

6 List two reasons why Kelly did not tell anyone about her idea. Use the text to support your answers.

    a. _____

    b. _____

7 List three things that happened in the story after Kelly decided to build a castle.

    a. _____

    b. _____

    c. _____

8 In the story, what was the purpose of the cans Kelly needed?

_____

_____

9 Write the sentence that helped you choose your answer for #8.

_____

_____

10 Complete this sentence: Castles were important because they helped keep people _____.

    (a) happy

    (b) safe

    (c) indoors

    (d) underground

11 What would be another good title for the story about "The School Project"?

_____

Explain why this title would be a good one for the story.

_____

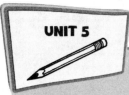

Time to Write!

Imagine you have a school project of your own to make. The teacher has asked you to design a clubhouse for yourself and your friends. Use the space below to describe the clubhouse. Then draw a picture of your clubhouse on the back of the page.

What size will the clubhouse be?	What will you use to make the clubhouse?

What are two special things that your clubhouse will have?

1. _____

2. _____

What color(s) will your clubhouse be?	Hang a sign outside your clubhouse. What will the sign say?

Where will you build your clubhouse?

Robot Pet

Cal walked through the toy store. He and his mother stopped when he saw a lot of children looking at something. When he got closer, he saw what they were looking at. All of the children were watching a robot dog.

Cal could not believe how real the dog looked. The man working in the store had the dog doing all types of tricks. The dog could speak. The dog could roll over. The dog could even shake hands.

The storeowner told everyone the dog would never make a mess in the house. The dog would go to sleep when told to go to sleep. Cal overheard another mother saying what an amazing pet the robot dog would make. The sign above the toy said the same thing: Take an amazing pet home today.

Later, Cal and his mother were driving home in their car. Cal was a little sad because his mother did not buy him a robot dog. He had not asked for one, but he felt sure she would get him the dog when she saw all the things it could do. He knew his mother had heard everything the man had said. She had to know a robot dog would make a great pet.

When they pulled into the driveway, Cal got out of the car. His two dogs ran to greet him. Their tails wagged, and Cal petted each one. He now knew why his mother had not bought him the robot dog. He already had two amazing pets!

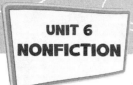
Robots

Robots are machines that can do special things. They work without help from anyone. Robots can be found in all shapes and sizes. Robots are used in many different places. They are used in many different ways. Some robots are used as far away as outer space. Others are used in people's homes. The science of robotics is truly amazing.

Some people's favorite robots are the ones found in movies or television. Many cartoon movies have robots in them, too. Most robots do not look like the ones found in movies or television. These pretend robots are not like the ones used in real life.

Robots that are used each day are made to help people. Robots are used in many different jobs. Sometimes, robots are used to help keep people safe. Some robots are sent where people cannot go. Robots have been to Mars, even though people have not. Robots on Mars can take pictures that help scientists study the planet. Robots will be used more and more. People already count on robots to help with many jobs. Maybe someday you will even have a robot that can clean your room!

Name _____   **Date** _____

The following pages have questions based on the texts from Unit 6.
You may look at the stories to help answer any questions. Use the
back of the page if you need extra space for writing your answers.

1 Why is a robot dog considered a perfect pet? Fill in **all** the answers that are correct.

(a) The robot dog never makes a mess.

(b) The robot dog never barks.

(c) The robot dog has an alarm.

(d) The robot dog goes to sleep when given the command.

2 What causes Cal to want a robot dog?

_____

_____

_____

3 What is the effect of seeing his two dogs?

_____

_____

_____

4 How are the two texts the same?

(a) They both talk about boys liking dogs.

(b) They both talk about robots.

(c) They both talk about the many ways a person can use a robot.

(d) The two have nothing in common.

5 Explain one way a robot can help keep someone safe. Use what you read from
the text to answer the question.

_____

_____

_____

_____

6 Which sentence from the story best explains why Cal is amazed by the robot dog?

(a) Cal could not believe how real the dog looked.

(b) Cal was a little sad because his mother did not buy him a robot dog.

(c) She had to know a robot dog would make a great pet.

(d) All of the children were watching a robot dog.

7 What is one amazing thing the toy dog could do?

_____

_____

_____

8 What is one job a robot can do that helps people?

_____

_____

_____

9 Why are robots sent to Mars?

_____

_____

_____

10 Which sentence from the story best helped you answer #9?

(a) Robots that are used each day are made to help people.

(b) Robots have been to Mars, even though people have not.

(c) Robots on Mars can take pictures that help scientists study the planet.

(d) Robots will be used more and more.

Time to Write!

Pretend you have a robot animal for sale. Write about the animal. Tell what it can do. Explain why you need to sell the robot. Use vivid words to describe the robot toy. Be sure to tell how much it costs. Then draw a picture of your robot animal.

FOR SALE

Dinosaurs Roar

Joey and Josh were happy to be visiting their uncle. The twins loved going to work with their Uncle Rick. Uncle Rick worked with a company that helped make movies. This time, the movie was all about dinosaurs. Uncle Rick told Joey and Josh that they were about to see some amazing things.

"Follow me, boys," Uncle Rick said to Joey and Josh. Joey and Josh walked through the door. They could not believe what they were seeing. In a large room on the other side of the door were dinosaurs. They were everywhere!

"Wow!" Joey said. "These dinosaurs look so real!"

"Did you help make these?" Josh asked his uncle.

Uncle Rick nodded. "Yes. These dinosaurs are part of a new movie. They need to look very real for the movie we are making. I am glad you both think they look like real dinosaurs."

Joey and Josh walked around and looked at the huge creatures up close. There was a Tyrannosaurus rex, a Stegosaurus, and even a Triceratops!

All of a sudden, the dinosaurs started to move. Joey and Josh both screamed and started to run, but there was no place to go. They were surrounded by moving dinosaurs. There was no sign of their uncle, but then they saw him. He was smiling. He didn't look scared at all.

"Relax, boys. I was just playing a joke. The dinosaurs are not alive. They are animatronics. They work like a remote-control car would. I can make them move and even roar. Would you two like to try?"

Uncle Rick was not surprised when both boys said yes!

Animatronics

Have you ever been to a museum and seen a dinosaur? Imagine if those large dinosaurs could move! Well, some museums have moving dinosaurs for people to see. They look very real to anyone who sees them. How do these creatures move? They use animatronics.

What is animatronics? It is a special type of technology that helps robots look real. People who make movies and television shows use this in many of their shows.

Some of these special robots move by remote control. These pretend animals work like a remote-control toy. Others are like puppets. People move them using large rods. Both ways make the animal look as though it is moving all by itself.

These robot animals look very real. People who make the ones you see in movies and television work hard to make the animals look real. Artists make a model of each animal. The pretend skin of each animal must be painted to look like the real animals. It takes many people to make these animals look and sound real. Their hard work pays off when everyone sees how real they look!

The following pages have questions based on the texts from Unit 7. You may look at the stories to help answer any questions. Use the back of the page if you need extra space for writing your answers.

1   Animatronics is a special type of technology . . .

     ⓐ that makes rockets go to the moon.

     ⓑ that helps robots look real.

     ⓒ that is only used in movies.

     ⓓ that is not real.

2   Which paragraph of the nonfiction text helped you to answer #1?

     ⓐ paragraph 1

     ⓑ paragraph 2

     ⓒ paragraph 3

     ⓓ paragraph 4

3   How are both stories the same?

     ⓐ They are both about animals.

     ⓑ They are both about dinosaurs.

     ⓒ They are both about animatronics.

     ⓓ They do not have anything in common.

4   Why are Joey and Josh amazed by the dinosaurs?

     ⓐ They are very large.

     ⓑ They look very real.

     ⓒ There are so many.

     ⓓ They get to keep one.

5   What do Joey and Josh do when the dinosaurs start to move?

_____

_____

_____

_____

6 What would you have done if you were with Joey and Josh when the dinosaurs started to move?

_____

_____

_____

7 Fill in the circles of **all** the things that are true about animatronics.

    (a) It helps robotic animals look real.

    (b) It is only used in movies.

    (c) Artists paint the pretend skin of robotic animals.

    (d) Animatronics is the science of making toys.

8 You answered #7 by circling things that are true. What does it mean if something is true and not false?

_____

_____

_____

9 Why might someone making a movie about dinosaurs use animatronics?

_____

_____

_____

10 What would be another good title for the story "Dinosaurs Roar"?

_____

Why did you choose this title?

_____

_____

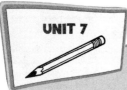

Time to Write!

Pretend you have discovered a new type of dinosaur. Use the space below to describe the dinosaur you have found. Write about the dinosaur on the lines.

What is the name of your new dinosaur?	What did your dinosaur eat?	Where did your dinosaur live?

Write two sentences to describe your dinosaur.

1. _____

_____

2. _____

_____

Compare your dinosaur to another animal.	What is one way they are alike?	What is one way they are different?
Animal: _____		

A New World

Alice was scared. Her family was moving to a new country. They were moving to America. Her father told her America was a land where dreams could come true. She hoped he was right. Her father's dream was to own his own land. Her mother's dream was to send Alice to a good school. Alice's dream was to see both of her parents happy. If moving to America would make them all happy, then she already loved the new country.

The night before the trip, Alice could barely sleep. The trip would take many weeks. She had never been on a boat. Her father told her the ride would be long. Her mother told her they would see a statue of a beautiful lady when they arrived. That is how they would know they had reached America.

Mary, a friend of Alice's, was also going on the trip. She was going with her grandmother. They were sailing to America to see her grandfather. Alice's friend had already been to America. This time, she and her grandmother would be staying. Alice was glad to know she would have a friend on the boat.

Thinking about the next day, Alice knew she was no longer scared. She smiled. She was sure all of her family's dreams were about to come true.

Ellis Island

Imagine you have just arrived in America. You have traveled by boat and have arrived in New York. One of the first things you see is the Statue of Liberty. It is a sign of hope for anyone coming to America. The statue is near another important place called Ellis Island. Ellis Island was the first place many people had to go to after they walked off their ships.

People who go to live in a new country are called immigrants. The immigrants who came through Ellis Island had to be seen by doctors. They could not stay until they did this. People wanting to go to America also had to answer a lot of questions. Some people were not able to stay. People who were very sick had to leave. People who had done bad things were turned away. However, most people were able to come into the country.

Today, people no longer go through Ellis Island to enter America. Visitors can still see Ellis Island. Visitors can also still see the Statue of Liberty.

UNIT 8 QUESTIONS

Name   **Date**

The following pages have questions based on the texts from Unit 8. You may look at the stories to help answer any questions. Use the back of the page if you need extra space for writing your answers.

1 In the story, Alice is scared. Which word means the opposite of *scared*?

(a) brave

(b) frightened

(c) upset

(d) afraid

2 What does Alice hope will happen in America?

(a) She wants to make new friends.

(b) She wants her parents to be happy.

(c) She wants to get a puppy.

(d) She wants to meet Mary's grandfather.

3 Alice loves her family. Write a sentence that explains how you know Alice loves her family.

_____

_____

_____

4 What is the same about both stories?

(a) They are both about people coming to America.

(b) They are both about the Statue of Liberty.

(c) They are both about people meeting new friends.

(d) There is nothing the same about the two stories.

5 What is one reason some people could not stay in America?

(a) They did not have money.

(b) They did not have any friends.

(c) They were very sick.

(d) They could not speak English.

6 This sentence is wrong. Change the words and write the sentence again to make it right.

People coming to America did not go through Ellis Island.

_____

_____

7 Alice wants everyone in her family to be happy. What do you think happens to Alice when she gets to America? Write two sentences to tell what happens next.

a. _____

_____

b. _____

_____

8 The Statue of Liberty and Ellis Island gave people coming to America _____.
- ⓐ hope
- ⓑ fear
- ⓒ sadness
- ⓓ joy

9 What does Alice's mother tell her she will see when they get to America?

_____

10 What would be another good title for the story "A New World"?

_____

Why did you choose this title for the story?

_____

_____

_____

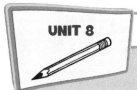

Time to Write!

Sometimes, doing something new can be hard. Pretend you are moving to a new school. What would you do to not be scared? What would you want to see or do at your new school?

Write a letter to someone in your class telling how you feel about moving to a new school. Be sure to explain whether you are scared or excited.

Having a friend is important. At your new school, what qualities would you want your new friends to have?

"Do you know what that is?" Jim's father asked.

He knew his dad was joking with him. Jim was looking through the glass at one of his favorite sea animals. He had never seen so many jellyfish up close. Getting to see the jellyfish was why Jim had wanted to come to the aquarium. Of course, there were many other things to see, but Jim could watch the jellyfish all day.

"I can't believe there are so many of them!" Jim said. "I wish I could touch them."

"You wouldn't want to do that," Jim's dad said. "Those jellyfish would sting you. Some of them can even poison you."

"I know, Dad," Jim said. "They just look as though they would be soft to touch."

Jim stepped up closer to the glass. He wanted to get a better look. He loved watching them move through the water. They looked like small umbrellas to him. He also liked all their colors. He did not know jellyfish came in so many different colors.

Other people were coming to see the jellyfish. Jim knew they had to go. His dad could tell he did not want to go yet.

"We will come back and look at the jellyfish before we go home," he promised Jim.

That was what Jim had hoped to hear!

Jellyfish

One amazing animal of the sea is the jellyfish. Jellyfish have bodies that look like they are made of jelly. They have two curved layers that are the top and bottom of the animal. These layers keep the body of the jellyfish safe.

Jellyfish swim by moving their bodies in and out. Tentacles hang down from the body of the jellyfish as it swims. They use the tentacles to catch their food. The tentacles hurt whatever they touch. Some jellyfish even have poison in their tentacles.

Jellyfish come in many colors and sizes. They can be pink, blue, or many other colors. Some jellyfish are tiny. They can be as small as a pea. Other jellyfish are large. They can be as long as a grown man.

No matter which jellyfish you see, they are all fun to watch as long as you remember not to get too close!

UNIT 9
QUESTIONS

Name   **Date**

The following pages have questions based on the texts from Unit 9. You may look at the stories to help answer any questions. Use the back of the page if you need extra space for writing your answers.

1 | What would be the best place to look to learn more about jellyfish?
- (a) a nonfiction book about jellyfish
- (b) a cartoon about going jellyfishing
- (c) a fiction story about a jellyfish who can't find its mother
- (d) a poem about a jellyfish

2 | From reading the story, what is NOT true about jellyfish?
- (a) They have two curved layers that are the top and bottom of the animal.
- (b) They come in many colors and sizes.
- (c) They stay on the bottom of the sea.
- (d) They use their tentacles to catch their food.

3 | Explain how you know your answer for #2 is not true about jellyfish.

_____

_____

_____

4 | Why does Jim want to go to the aquarium?
- (a) He wants to see the sharks.
- (b) He wants to see the dolphins.
- (c) He wants to see the penguins.
- (d) He wants to see the jellyfish.

5 | What can you say is true about Jim and his father?
- (a) Jim's father wants to make Jim happy.
- (b) Jim and his father do not like the aquarium.
- (c) Jim and his dad wish they had gone to the zoo.
- (d) Jim and his father are ready to go home.

6 Why does Jim have to stop looking at the jellyfish?

_____

_____

7 Compare another animal to a jellyfish. Animal: _____
Write one way they are the same.

_____

_____

Write one way they are NOT the same.

_____

_____

8 Complete this sentence: Jellyfish catch their food by using their _____.

    (a) arms
    (b) jelly
    (c) colors
    (d) tentacles

9 Write the sentence from the story that helped you answer #8.

_____

_____

10 What do both stories have in common?

    (a) They are both about going to the aquarium.
    (b) They are both about jellyfish.
    (c) They are both about a trip to the sea.
    (d) There is nothing the same about them.

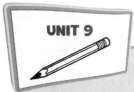

Time to Write!

Pretend you are a jellyfish! You swim in the sea. You have long tentacles. You see all the other animals in the water.

Write about your day as a jellyfish. What do you do? What do you see? How does it feel to be a jellyfish? What do you look like?

_____

_____

_____

_____

_____

_____

_____

_____

_____

_____

_____

Look at the picture of the jellyfish in the aquarium. What question would you like to ask the jellyfish? Write your question below.

_____

_____

_____

_____

Winter Fun

Mike loved winter. Each January, it would snow. Sometimes, it would snow a lot. Sometimes, it would only snow a little. But he always knew he would get to see some snow. Mike loved playing in the snow in winter.

Mike's grandmother lived where it never snowed. She had moved to Florida when Mike was only a baby. He knew she loved the warm weather. He loved to visit her at the beach, but he wished she did not live so far away. He wished she could come and play in the snow with him.

When Mike looked out the window, he saw that the snow was starting to fall from the sky. As he watched the snow fall, he had an idea. He asked his mom if he could use her camera on her phone. He took a picture of the snow. He sent it to his grandmother. She took a picture of the sand. She sent it to him.

They may not be able to be together, but Mike was glad they could still share things with each other.

The First Month

January is the first month of the year. Where did the month get its name? The word *January* came from a Roman god named Janus. Many years ago, the Romans believed in different gods. Each god had special powers. Janus was one of the Roman gods. The word *January* comes from his name. The god had two faces. With one face, he could see the past. With the other face, he could see the future.

There are two important holidays in January. New Year's Day is on January 1. People have parties and do special things to welcome in the new year. People also celebrate the birthday of Martin Luther King, Jr. Martin Luther King, Jr. worked hard to see that everyone was treated fairly. He wanted people to be kind to one another.

For some people, January is a very cold month. For other people, January is a very warm month. Are the thirty-one days of January cold or hot where you live? Either way, January is an important month of the year!

UNIT 10 QUESTIONS

Name _____   **Date** _____

The following pages have questions based on the texts from Unit 10. You may look at the stories to help answer any questions. Use the back of the page if you need extra space for writing your answers.

1 Why can't Mike see his grandmother?

(a) Mike is blind.

(b) She does not live near Mike.

(c) Mike does not know where she is.

(d) She does not want to see him.

2 Why does Mike take pictures of the snow?

(a) He wants his grandmother to see the snow.

(b) He wants to show the snow to his mother.

(c) He likes taking pictures of the snow.

(d) He likes playing with his mother's camera.

3 Fill in the circle of the sentence that is true.

(a) January is always a cold month.

(b) January is always a hot month.

(c) There are no holidays in January.

(d) January is named after a Roman god.

4 Write about one of the two holidays in January.

_____

_____

_____

5 Mike wants to share things with his grandmother. Write a sentence that tells how Mike feels about his grandmother.

_____

_____

_____

_____

6 Which word makes the sentence NOT true? Circle the word.

For all people, January is a very cold month.

7 Which sentence(s) in the story helped you find the answer to #6?

_____

_____

_____

_____

8 Describe the god Janus.

_____

_____

_____

_____

9 Why did Mike's grandmother send him a picture of the sand?

_____

_____

_____

_____

10 How do you know Mike likes spending time with his grandmother?

_____

_____

_____

_____

Time to Write!

Many people like to play in the snow. Make a list of things you might need if you were going to build a snowman. Don't forget to include what you might wear to play outside in the snow!

_____

_____

_____

_____

_____

_____

Many people like to play in the sand. Make a list of things you might need if you were going to go to the beach and build a sandcastle. Don't forget to include what you might wear on your day at the beach.

_____

_____

_____

_____

_____

The Playful Giants

"Let's go this way, Daddy," Lynn said.

Lynn and her father were at the zoo. Lynn loved seeing the monkeys, the tigers, and the lions. She loved seeing all the animals. But she still had not seen her favorite animal. She wanted to see the elephants.

Her father took her hand. They walked down the path that had a picture of an elephant on a sign. At the end of the path was a large field. There were the elephants!

Lynn could not remember ever seeing such a big animal! The giraffes had been tall. The snakes had been long. But the elephants were big all over. Even their ears were big!

As Lynn watched the elephants, one of the smaller ones went over to the water. He filled his trunk. Lynn watched him spray the water all over the elephant that was beside him. He was playing!

That was why she loved the elephants the best. They were big, and they were a lot of fun!

The Mighty Elephant

The elephant is the largest land animal. Some whales are larger than the elephant. But whales live in water and not on land. Giraffes are taller than the elephant, but they are not as big. The elephant is also the only animal that has a trunk for a nose. The long trunk is like an extra hand for the elephant!

There are two types of elephants. There are African elephants and Asian elephants. African elephants are larger. They have dark gray skin. They also have tusks. The Asian elephants have light gray skin. The ears of the Asian elephants are not as big. Some of the Asian elephants have tusks, but not all do. Their tusks are much smaller than the African elephant's tusks.

Today, people want to make sure elephants are kept safe. There are places for them to live where no one is allowed to hunt. Elephants are hunted for their tusks. People want the tusks because they are made of ivory.

It would be awful to have a world with no elephants. With people watching over this animal and its habitat, the mighty elephant should be around forever.

Asian Elephant　　　　**African Elephant**

The following pages have questions based on the texts from Unit 11. You may look at the stories to help answer any questions. Use the back of the page if you need extra space for writing your answers.

1 From reading the stories, which sentence do you know is true?

   (a) The elephant is larger than any other animal that lives on land.

   (b) The elephant is larger than any animal that lives on land or in the water.

   (c) The elephant is the largest of all the animals.

   (d) The elephant is one of the smallest animals.

2 Which sentence from the story helped you find the answer to #1?

_____

_____

_____

3 Why does Lynn love elephants more than any other animal at the zoo?

   (a) They are so big.

   (b) They are big, and they like to have fun.

   (c) They are very shy.

   (d) They have large ears.

4 If Lynn went to another zoo, which animals would she most likely want to see?

   (a) whales

   (b) tigers

   (c) snakes

   (d) elephants

5 The story says that people want to keep the elephant's habitat safe. What does the word *habitat* mean?

_____

_____

_____

6 Lynn likes elephants the best. Write two reasons why she likes elephants so much.

a. _____

_____

b. _____

_____

7 Write one adjective to describe the elephant.

_____

8 Write a word that is the opposite of the word you wrote for #7.

_____

9 "The Playful Giants" is the title of the story. What does the title mean?

_____

_____

_____

10 List three things that happened in the story "The Playful Giants." Write them in the order they happened.

First, _____

_____

Next, _____

_____

Finally, _____

_____

Time to Write!

The circus is coming to your town! Everyone wants to see the elephants. Use the space and the picture below to create a flyer that will tell everyone about the circus.

Be sure to tell the following:

- When the circus is coming
- Where the circus will be
- What everyone will see
- How much it costs

Something Extra: Color the picture when you are finished writing.

A Magical Place

Jack could not believe it. He was at Disney World! He was on the trip with his aunt, his uncle, and his cousin Dan. He had never been to Disney World, but Dan and his parents had been there many times. Dan smiled when he saw how happy Jack was.

"What do you want to do first?" Dan asked Jack.

"Everything!" Jack said.

"Let's go on some rides," Dan said.

Jack smiled. "That is a great idea."

Jack and Dan rode the swings. They rode some water rides. Then they were ready to ride a roller coaster.

"I have never been on a roller coaster," Jack told Dan.

"Are you scared?" Dan asked Jack.

"I am a little scared," Jack said.

"I will ride with you," Dan told Jack.

The two boys got on the ride. The ride began to move. Jack yelled as they went up and down the hills. Dan yelled, too.

When they got off the ride, both boys were smiling.

"What do you want to do next?" Dan asked Jack.

"What do you think?" Jack said.

The two boys ran to get back in the line.

A Man with a Dream

Walt Disney was born in 1901. He made the cartoon character Mickey Mouse for everyone to love. Walt grew up on a farm. When he became a teenager, he began to study art. He started drawing cartoons for other people to use to help sell things.

Walt Disney wanted to make movies. When he was older, he set up his own movie studio. His movies were cartoons. Mickey Mouse was the star! Walt became the voice for Mickey. Later, he would create many other characters besides his much-loved Mickey Mouse. Disney's first long film was *Snow White and the Seven Dwarfs*. Children today still enjoy watching this movie.

Today, the company that was started by Walt Disney still makes movies. It also owns theme parks, where people can visit and see many of Walt Disney's ideas. There are rides, shows, and many other things at each park for everyone to enjoy. Many of the rides at the parks are based on the movies he made. But it is always Mickey Mouse that everyone knows and loves!

UNIT 12 QUESTIONS

Name _____ **Date** _____

The following pages have questions based on the texts from Unit 12. You may look at the stories to help answer any questions. Use the back of the page if you need extra space for writing your answers.

1 How do you know Jack is happy to be on the trip?

    (a) He wants to do everything.

    (b) He is not crying.

    (c) He wants to call his mother.

    (d) He wants to get something to eat.

2 Why was Jack scared about riding the roller coaster?

    (a) He thought it was too high.

    (b) He thought it was too fast.

    (c) He had never been on a roller coaster before.

    (d) He thought he would have to ride it by himself.

3 Walt Disney is most likely best known because of which cartoon character?

    (a) Snow White

    (b) Mickey Mouse

    (c) Donald Duck

    (d) Walt Disney

4 Write a sentence from the stories that helped you to answer #3.

_____

_____

_____

5 What did Walt Disney really want to do?

    (a) He wanted to draw cartoons.

    (b) He wanted to have his own business.

    (c) He wanted to make movies.

    (d) He wanted to stop making cartoons.

6 Do you think Dan had been on a roller coaster before? Why or why not?

_____

_____

_____

7 Which word best describes Walt Disney?

(a) creative

(b) angry

(c) nice

(d) shy

8 Explain why you chose your answer for #7.

_____

_____

_____

9 Will Jack most likely want to visit the theme park again? How do you know?

_____

_____

_____

10 What would be another good title for the story "A Magical Place"? Why would this be a good title for the story?

_____

_____

_____

_____

Time to Write!

You have been asked to make a new cartoon character. Use the space below to draw your idea. Then answer the questions.

1 What is the name of your character? _____

2 Use three words to describe your character.

    a. _____

    b. _____

    c. _____

3 What makes your character special or different?

_____

_____

4 What does your character like to do?

_____

_____

Something Extra: On the back of the page, draw a friend for your new character. Write about your second character underneath the picture.

Opening Night

Don and Libby were ready for the curtain to go up. The twins were about to be in their first school play. The play was about a farmer and his talking animals.

The brother and sister knew their parents were at the school. They had seats near the stage. They had heard Don and Libby talk a lot about the play. They knew the twins each knew their parts. They could not wait to see them onstage.

The curtain opened. Don and Libby stepped to the front of the stage. Don was dressed as a cow. Libby was dressed as a pig.

Don said, "Moo, moo, moo."

Libby said, "Oink, oink, oink."

Don told Libby to "mooove" out of his way. She was *hogging* the stage.

The crowd laughed after Don said his lines.

Libby told Don that his lines were *udderly* bad.

Everyone laughed again as Don and Libby went back and joined the other students.

Don and Libby went to stand by the barn that had been painted on the back wall. They saw their parents in the crowd. They were taking pictures with their phones. Judging by the size of the grins on their parents' faces, they knew their parents liked the play. Being an animal for the night was a lot of fun!

Are the Aliens Here?

Before there was television, people listened to the radio at night. Families would gather around the radio and listen to their favorite shows. People would listen to live radio shows or plays. This means the shows were happening as the people were listening.

Many years ago, there was a show on the radio that scared some people. The show was about aliens coming to Earth. The play was made to sound as though it was a real news story. People thought aliens from Mars had landed on Earth. In the play, the aliens were very mean. Many people did not understand that the radio play was made-up. People were scared. They ran from their houses. They hid. They called their friends. They even began calling the police, trying to get help.

The people who put on the radio play were very sorry that they had made everyone worry. They explained they did not know people would think the show was real. Today, with computers, everyone can find out what is going on very quickly. It is hard to imagine a time when people did not always know what was happening.

The following pages have questions based on the texts from Unit 13. You may look at the stories to help answer any questions. Use the back of the page if you need extra space for writing your answers.

1 Which sentence best shows that everyone is enjoying the play Don and Libby are doing?

   (a) The brother and sister knew their parents were at the school.

   (b) They could not wait to see them onstage.

   (c) Don and Libby stepped to the front of the stage.

   (d) Everyone laughed again as Don and Libby went back and joined the other students.

2 What is one way the two stories are alike?

   (a) Both were about plays that were being done live.

   (b) The people listening to both plays were smiling and laughing.

   (c) Both plays had aliens.

   (d) Don and Libby were in both plays.

3 Which sentence helps you know Don and Libby are not nervous about the play?

   (a) The twins were about to be in their first school play.

   (b) Don and Libby went to stand by the barn that had been painted on the back wall.

   (c) Don and Libby were ready for the curtain to go up.

   (d) Being an animal for the night was a lot of fun!

4 Which word best describes how people felt while hearing the radio play about the aliens?

   (a) silly

   (b) happy

   (c) lonely

   (d) scared

5 Which sentence from the story helped you to answer #4?

_____

_____

_____

_____

6 Write two things that happened when people were listening to the radio play about the aliens.

a. _____

_____

b. _____

_____

7 Explain why people were afraid when they listened to the radio play about the aliens.

_____

_____

8 If Don and Libby were real people, would they have been living when the radio play happened? How do you know?

_____

_____

9 Write two words that best tell how Don and Libby felt about being in a play.

a. _____

b. _____

10 Don and Libby had never been in a play, but they did not seem nervous about doing the play. Think of something new you have done. Write about what you did, and explain how it made you feel. Were you scared or nervous? Was it fun?

_____

_____

_____

_____

_____

Time to Write!

Use the space below to write a short play. The two characters have already been chosen. Have the sun and moon talking to each other. Think about what they will say to each other before you begin writing. Use the back of the page if you need more space.

Title: _____

Sun: _____

_____

_____

Moon: _____

_____

_____

Sun: _____

_____

_____

Moon: _____

_____

_____

The End

What Goes Up Must Come Down

The kite was stuck.

Emma and Conner had been flying their kites all morning. The wind had been just right. Emma's kite was in the shape of a diamond. Conner's kite looked like a box. Emma's kite flew straight up. It went very high. Emma loved watching her bright yellow kite. Conner's kite would dip and sway. It did not go as high as Emma's. His kite looked like a rainbow in the sky. It had many different colors on each side.

As they were flying their kites, Conner's suddenly tilted on its side. Then it began to fall. Emma did not know how to help Conner. They both watched as Conner's kite fell and landed in a tree. Now his kite was stuck.

Emma began winding up her string. She brought her kite out of the sky. She wanted to help get Conner's kite out of the tree, but she didn't know how they could reach the top of such a large tree.

The two friends were standing in Emma's front yard, staring at the tree when they heard the honk of a horn. They looked over and saw a bright red fire truck pulling up to the front of the house. It was Conner's uncle.

"Looks like you could use some help," Conner's uncle said.

Conner's uncle and the other men on his truck jumped out and began pulling out the ladder. He climbed to the top and got the kite for Conner.

Emma and Conner thanked the men for their help. Conner's uncle asked them if they would like to see the truck, but just then, an alarm went off.

"Sorry, kids," Conner's uncle said. "Right now, we have to go and help someone else."

The History of Kites

Kites have been around for many thousands of years. People believe the first kites probably came from China. Today, people fly kites to have fun. Years ago, though, people used them for other reasons. In battle, the Chinese soldiers would tie pipes made of bamboo to kites. The wind would blow through the pipes. The wind would make the sound of a whistle. The noise would scare the other people, and they would run away from the odd noise coming from the sky.

Benjamin Franklin used a kite for his experiment. He tied a metal key to the string of his kite. He flew the kite during a thunderstorm. He used the kite to help prove his theory about lightning and electricity.

Kites were also used to help people learn to fly. Kites are, in fact, the oldest type of aircraft. The Wright brothers used the box kite to help them design their airplanes. The Wright brothers were the first people to be able to control a plane while flying it in the air.

Kites are an important part of history, but they are also fun for people today to fly and to watch. On almost any windy day, you will see someone, somewhere, flying a kite.

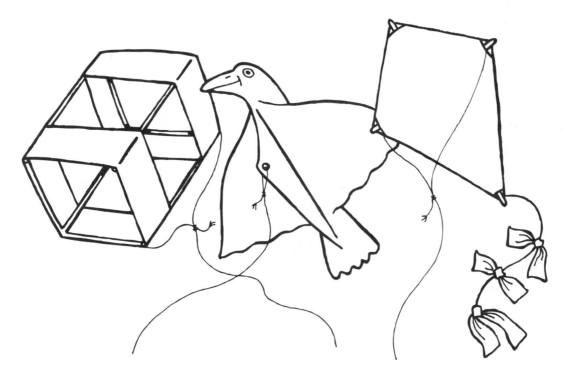

UNIT 14 QUESTIONS

Name	Date

The following pages have questions based on the texts from Unit 14. You may look at the stories to help answer any questions. Use the back of the page if you need extra space for writing your answers.

1 How did the early Chinese use kites?

  (a) in festivals

  (b) for birthdays

  (c) in battles

  (d) for school

2 How is Conner's uncle able to reach the kite that is stuck?

  (a) He is a very tall man.

  (b) He climbs the tree.

  (c) He climbs on the shoulders of another person.

  (d) He uses the ladder from the fire truck.

3 How do you know Emma is worried about Conner's kite?

_____

_____

_____

_____

4 What is the same about the two stories?

  (a) They are both about the importance of helping others.

  (b) They are both about kites.

  (c) They both have a story about Benjamin Franklin.

  (d) They both tell how to make your own kite.

5 Why didn't Conner's uncle show the truck to Emma and Conner?

  (a) Conner's uncle had to go home.

  (b) Conner's uncle forgot to bring the key.

  (c) Conner's uncle was not allowed to have kids on the truck.

  (d) Conner's uncle and the firemen had to go and help someone else.

6 Why were people afraid of the kites that the early Chinese flew?

_____

_____

_____

7 Who are the two main characters in the story "What Goes Up Must Come Down"?

_____ **and** _____

8 Which answer choice best completes this sentence?

The Wright brothers used a _____ to help them make a better airplane.

- (a) bamboo stick
- (b) key
- (c) box kite
- (d) fire truck

9 Write the sentence from the story that helped you answer #8.

_____

_____

_____

10 Were kites important in the past? Explain your answer.

_____

_____

_____

_____

_____

Time to Write!

Explain what is happening in each picture. Write your sentences on the lines.

_____

_____

_____

_____

_____

_____

Ann's Pets

Ann had two pet rabbits. One was named Sally, and the other one was named Tammy. The rabbits were a gift from Ann's grandmother. She lived on a farm. She gave Ann lots of things, but the rabbits were Ann's favorite present.

One thing Ann loved to do was feed her rabbits. She would go out to the small house her dad had made for them and feed them special treats she got at the pet store. The rabbits also loved it when she gave them fresh carrots to eat.

One day when Ann went out to feed her pets, she saw that the door to the rabbit's house was not closed. When Ann went to look for her rabbits, they were gone! Ann began to call for the rabbits. She shouted their names. She put out food for the rabbits, hoping they would get hungry and come back to eat. No matter what Ann did, the rabbits did not come back.

That night, Ann cried herself to sleep. She was so sad. She did not know where her rabbits were. She did not know what would happen to Sally and Tammy. She wanted to see her rabbits again, but she was afraid she never would.

The next morning, Ann went back out into the yard to look one last time. She could not believe her eyes! Waiting beside the food bowl were her two rabbits. They were back, and they were hungry! The rabbits ate every last bit of food that Ann put in their dish.

Ann did not know where her pets had been. She was just so happy they had come back to her.

Making Peter Rabbit

Peter Rabbit has been a favorite rabbit in children's books for many years. Thanks to Beatrix Potter, children all over the world have come to know all about the tales of Peter Rabbit and his friends.

When Beatrix Potter was a little girl, she went to school at her home. She learned about many different things. One subject she was very good at was art. She wanted to be good at art so she could draw pictures to go with her many stories.

Beatrix Potter first began writing for a little boy she knew who was sick. He loved the stories she wrote for him. She then put all the stories together into a book.

One day, a company that made books saw her stories and the book she had made. They wanted everyone to be able to read her wonderful stories and see her beautiful pictures. They began to help her sell her stories about Peter Rabbit.

Today, people all over the world have heard about the adventures of Peter Rabbit and his many friends.

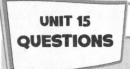

UNIT 15 QUESTIONS

Name   **Date**

The following pages have questions based on the texts from Unit 15. You may look at the stories to help answer any questions. Use the back of the page if you need extra space for writing your answers.

1 How does Ann feel about the gifts from her grandmother?

    (a) She likes the things her grandmother gives her.

    (b) She does not like the gifts her grandmother gives her.

    (c) She only likes some of the gifts her grandmother gives her.

    (d) She never gets any gifts from her grandmother.

2 *The Tale of Peter Rabbit* was first written for . . .

    (a) a classroom of students.

    (b) a sick child.

    (c) a friend as a gift.

    (d) a project for school.

3 Which sentence from the story best helped you to answer #2?

_____

_____

_____

_____

4 Which word best shows how Ann feels when she sees her rabbits the next day?

    (a) joyful

    (b) sad

    (c) sick

    (d) sleepy

5 From what you read, what do you know is true about Beatrix Potter?

    (a) She took many art classes.

    (b) She wrote the stories for her books and drew the pictures.

    (c) She had lots of friends at school.

    (d) She was very shy.

6 Do you think Ann will do anything new to help keep her rabbits safe? Explain your answer.

_____

_____

_____

7 Why does Ann cry herself to sleep?

_____

_____

_____

8 What is the same about the two stories you just read?

_____

_____

_____

9 If you wanted to know more about Beatrix Potter, where would you look?
- (a) a dictionary
- (b) a nonfiction book about Beatrix Potter
- (c) a coloring book
- (d) a book with stories about Peter Rabbit

10 How would Ann most likely feel about the stories in *The Tale of Peter Rabbit*? Explain your answer.

_____

_____

_____

_____

Time to Write!

Write your own story about a rabbit named Peter. Use the lines below to write about the fun times he has.

_____

_____

_____

_____

_____

_____

_____

_____

_____

_____

_____

_____

_____

_____

Something Extra: On the back of the page, draw a picture of you with your new rabbit friend.

Boy in the Suit

Jake was excited to be at his brother's football game. He could not wait to see his brother. He had not been able to come to see his brother's first game because he had been home sick. He was glad he was able to be at this game. All of his friends told him what a good job his brother did at the last game. He could not wait to see it for himself.

The band began to play music. The cheerleaders began to shout. Jake knew it was almost time for everyone to stand up and cheer for the team as they ran out onto the field. Jake could not wait to see Ryan.

His eyes searched the field. Then he spotted him. His brother was running all over the field. Everyone was cheering for him, and the game hadn't even begun! His brother ran up to the seats, and everyone cheered. He ran back over to the circle of boys on the field, and the team looked glad to see him. Then he came back to the crowd, and everyone cheered again.

Jake knew lots of his friends' brothers played in the game but not his brother. His brother wore a bear costume and was the mascot for the school. Jake thought his brother's job was just as important as the boys who were playing on the field. As he watched the crowd, he knew what his friends said was true. His brother was awesome, but he already knew that!

Bears are mammals. There are many different types of bears. Bears have large bodies and strong legs. They are covered in fur. The fur on the body of a bear comes in different colors, but most bears are shades of black, brown, or white. The only totally white bear is the polar bear.

Bears live in different habitats. The polar bears' white fur helps them to blend in with the snow and ice in their habitat. Most polar bears are found in the Arctic. It is cold all year long in this area. North America also has bears. Brown bears can be found there. Brown bears are also found in other parts of the world. They live in forests and sometimes areas that do not have as many trees. Panda bears are found in China. These bears need to be near their food. Panda bears live in the bamboo forests found naturally in China.

People need to do what they can to help keep all bears safe. The habitats of these bears are disappearing. Changes in the weather are hurting the habitat of the polar bears. The weather is becoming warmer. Pandas are beginning to lose their food source. The bamboo forests of China are beginning to disappear. Bears that live in the woods are also hurt as more and more trees are being cut down.

UNIT 16 QUESTIONS

Name

Date

The following pages have questions based on the texts from Unit 16. You may look at the stories to help answer any questions. Use the back of the page if you need extra space for writing your answers.

1 How do you know Jake's brother is NOT a football player?

(a) He is wearing a bear costume.

(b) He is sitting on the bench.

(c) He has a broken leg.

(d) He is not at the game.

2 What does the word *searched* mean in the sentence below?

His eyes searched the field.

(a) reached for

(b) looked around

(c) went after

(d) looked away from

3 Why are changes in the weather hurting the habitat of polar bears?

(a) The weather is getting too cold.

(b) The weather is getting too warm.

(c) It is snowing too much.

(d) It is too windy.

4 In the story "Boy in the Suit," which word best describes the bear?

(a) mean

(b) silly

(c) sad

(d) scary

5 Think of a word that would describe a brown bear found in North America. Write your word on the line.

_____

6 Write two or three sentences telling what the story "Boy in a Suit" is about.

_____

_____

_____

_____

7 If the story "Bears" was not labeled as a nonfiction story, how would you know the story is nonfiction?

_____

_____

8 Write two things that happened *after* Jake saw his brother on the field.

a. _____

b. _____

9 What do the two stories have in common?
- (a) family
- (b) football
- (c) weather
- (d) bears

10 Write a sentence from each story that helps show you have the right answer for #9.

"The Boy in the Suit": _____

_____

"Bears": _____

_____

Time to Write!

This poor teddy bear has been pushed to the bottom of the toy box and forgotten. Write a story about the bear. Tell how he feels. Explain why someone should find him and play with him again. Help the teddy bear have a happy ending!

Title: _____

_____

_____

_____

_____

_____

_____

_____

_____

_____

Open Wide!

Ben had never been to the dentist before. He knew his older sister Jane had been to the dentist many times. She always came home with a new toothbrush and a new tube of toothpaste whenever she went. She never had any problems at the dentist. She told Ben she always took care of her teeth and that Ben should, too.

He had tried to listen to what Jane told him to do. He knew she was right. Sometimes when he was sleepy, it was hard to remember to brush his teeth before he went to bed. He loved eating sweet foods. He did not always brush his teeth like he should. He did not know what the dentist would say. He was worried. He hoped everything would be okay after the dentist looked at his teeth.

A woman came and took Ben back to a room. Ben sat in a chair, and the chair tilted backwards. He opened his mouth so she could see inside. She talked to him about school and his family as she worked on his teeth. She smiled a lot, and Ben thought she was very nice. When she was finished, the dentist also came in to see Ben. Her name was Dr. Brown.

Dr. Brown also wanted to see inside Ben's mouth. Ben crossed his fingers and hoped everything would be good. When she was done, she had Ben sit up in his chair. She told Ben that his teeth looked good but that he needed to make sure he brushed his teeth at least two times each day. She told him if he would take care of his teeth, he would probably never have any problems.

Ben could not believe it. He had gone to the dentist for the very first time, and everything was great. He could not wait to tell Jane!

Getting the Perfect Smile

Today, people have lots of ways to get a perfect smile. Having a perfect smile is, in part, due to the work done by dentists. Dentists show children and adults how to care for their teeth. They make sure everyone cleans their teeth and takes good care of them. People can even get braces to help make a perfect smile!

People were not always as lucky with their teeth as they are now. People have always had problems with their teeth. There have not always been dentists who could help fix those problems. If a tooth was bad, it would be pulled. If you had lived in America in the early 1700s, you would have had very few teeth left by the time you were twenty!

Today, people go to visit the dentist at an office. Years ago, a person would travel to a town to visit people who needed help with their teeth. The person would not try to fix the tooth. He would just pull out the person's tooth!

People are lucky because today much more is known about how to help people have strong and healthy teeth. If you are lucky, the only teeth you will lose are the baby ones!

UNIT 17 QUESTIONS

Name _____ **Date** _____

The following pages have questions based on the texts from Unit 17. You may look at the stories to help answer any questions. Use the back of the page if you need extra space for writing your answers.

1 How does Ben feel about going to the dentist at the beginning of the story?

   (a) He feels happy.

   (b) He feels nervous.

   (c) He feels fine.

   (d) He feels sad.

2 Which paragraph best shows how Ben feels before the dentist looks at his teeth?

   (a) paragraph 1

   (b) paragraph 2

   (c) paragraph 3

   (d) paragraph 4

3 If Ben had lived in the 1700s, what would the dentist most likely do if he had a tooth that hurt him?

   (a) The dentist would do nothing.

   (b) The dentist would pull out the tooth.

   (c) The dentist would send him to another doctor.

   (d) The dentist would get his parents to take care of the tooth.

4 Which teeth should a person lose?

   (a) his or her adult teeth

   (b) his or her baby teeth

   (c) his or her front teeth

   (d) all of his or her adult teeth

5 Write the sentence from the story that helped you to answer #4.

_____

_____

_____

_____

6 How will Ben most likely feel about going to the dentist the next time?

_____

_____

_____

7 Which statement is true about the history of dentistry?

(a) Long ago, most people with any type of teeth problem had their teeth pulled.

(b) Dentists tried to save each person's teeth.

(c) Dentists used braces made of wood to help make crooked teeth straight.

(d) People long ago did not have problems with their teeth because they did not eat lots of sugar.

8 Write three sentences telling what Jane might have said to Ben when she heard about his trip to the dentist.

a. _____

_____

b. _____

_____

c. _____

_____

9 George Washington, the first president of the United States of America, lived in the 1700s. What might be true about his teeth?

_____

_____

_____

10 Which story best helped you to answer #9? Circle your choice.

a. "Getting the Perfect Smile"   b. "Open Wide!"

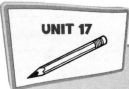

Time to Write!

Make a list of words and phrases that could be used to describe someone's perfect smile. The first one has been done for you.

1. ___snowy white___   4. _____

2. _____   5. _____

3. _____   6. _____

Draw a picture of a perfect smile. Write two sentences to tell about your picture.

```




```

_____

_____

_____

_____

_____

_____

_____

_____

The Accident

Mitch's arm was really hurting him. He wasn't sure if he could make it home. He had been riding his bike all day. He loved the way the wind blew his hair and made him feel cool even though the sun was hot. He could ride his bike all day and never get tired. He wasn't tired now, but his arm hurt him a lot. He could hardly hold the handlebars.

One of Mitch's favorite spots to ride his bike was in a field next to his house. There was a small hill he would climb with his bike. Then he would race down the hill. He always wore his helmet when he rode. He knew an accident could happen, and he did not want to hurt his head. Too bad, he thought, that he did not have something to protect his arm. He had been riding down the hill when his front tire slipped. His bike began to shake. The bike flipped, and Mitch was stuck underneath the bike. His arm hit against the ground hard. That is when his arm started to hurt.

Mitch's mother saw Mitch riding very slowly up the drive. She ran out to meet him. She could tell something was wrong. She looked at his arm and told him she was worried it might be broken. They would have to go to the doctor to see what was wrong. She hugged him close and told him not to worry. They would do whatever they needed to help him get better.

Mitch looked at his bike parked in his yard as the car pulled away from his house. He didn't know if he would need a cast, but he knew he would ride his bike again soon.

Bones: Just Doing Their Job

A human's skeleton does many things. It helps the body to move. It also protects parts of the body. The bones help keep the inside organs of people and animals safe. The skull protects the brain. The ribs protect the heart and lungs. All the bones have an important part in helping the skeleton do its job.

Bones come in many shapes and sizes. Think about how tall some people are. Think about how small other people are. The sizes of their bones would be very different. The largest land animals to ever live were the dinosaurs. Most dinosaurs had huge bones. Bones also look very different from one another. The bone in a person's jaw looks nothing like the bone in a person's leg. But each bone is very important.

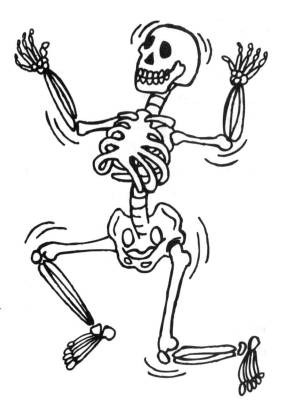

What are the smallest bones in a person's body? The three smallest bones are very tiny. They are in a person's ear. The bones have an important job because they help a person to hear sounds. The three small bones are called the hammer, the anvil, and the stirrup. The bones are called these names because of their unusual shapes.

Big or little bones can break. Most bones can heal, but it takes time for a bone to become better. Most skeletons do their job very well, which is to help you move and to keep you safe from injuries.

UNIT 18 QUESTIONS

Name _____ **Date** _____

The following pages have questions based on the texts from Unit 18. You may look at the stories to help answer any questions. Use the back of the page if you need extra space for writing your answers.

1 From the story, you can tell that Mitch . . .

 (a) will never ride his bike again.

 (b) will ride his bike again as soon as he can.

 (c) will give his bike away.

 (d) will only ride his bike if someone is with him.

2 Why was Mitch having trouble holding the bike's handlebar?

 (a) He was in a lot of pain.

 (b) The handlebars were wet.

 (c) He was very tired.

 (d) The handlebars were bent.

3 The skeleton is important because . . .

 (a) it helps protect parts of the body and helps it to move.

 (b) it helps the body to move and helps the heart to beat.

 (c) it helps the heart to beat and protects parts of the body.

 (d) it helps the body to get rest.

4 Which paragraph in "Bones: Just Doing Their Job" helped you to answer #3?

 (a) paragraph 1

 (b) paragraph 2

 (c) paragraph 3

 (d) the title

5 What does Mitch's mother think is wrong with his arm?

_____

_____

_____

_____

6 Circle the part of the skeleton that keeps the heart and lungs safe. Explain how you knew the answer.

_____

_____

_____

_____

_____

_____

7 List in order what happens in the story. Use the numbers 1 to 4. Put 1 by what happened first and 4 by what happened last.

_____ Mitch was riding down the hill.

_____ Mitch's mother put him into the car.

_____ Mitch made it home.

_____ Mitch's bike flipped.

8 How does Mitch feel about riding his bike?

_____

_____

9 If you were Mitch's mother, would you let him ride his bicycle again? Circle _yes_ or _no_. Explain your answer.

Yes / No because _____

_____.

10 Where are the smallest bones in the body?

ⓐ the ear

ⓑ the nose

ⓒ the skull

ⓓ the foot

Time to Write!

Mitch was hurt riding his bike. Think about a time something bad happened to you. Write a letter to someone you know and tell him or her what happened. Tell how you felt. How did things get better?

Dear _____,

I can't believe this happened to me. I

_____

_____

_____

_____

_____

_____

_____

_____

Thanks for letting me tell you what happened to me.

From,

Creepy Crawly

The night was perfect. There was no rain in sight. Pam and her best friend Kristy were going to camp outside in Pam's backyard. Pam's dad had put up the tent for the girls. Both girls had a sleeping bag and a flashlight. Pam's parents had left all the lights on at the back of the house so the girls could see everything better. They told the girls not to stay outside if they were worried. They could come inside if they got scared. Both girls said they would be fine.

At first, everything was great. The girls ate hot dogs and laughed and told stories. They felt so grown-up staying outside all by themselves. The tent was warm and cozy. They were glad they were spending the night with each other. Pam always loved spending time with her best friend.

After a few hours had passed, both girls began to get sleepy. They decided to go ahead and go to bed. They unzipped their sleeping bags and crawled inside. Kristy turned off her flashlight. Pam was just about to turn off her flashlight when she saw something outside the tent. It was a huge spider!

Pam and Kristy screamed. The spider crawled quickly to the door. The door was still unzipped. The girls just knew the giant spider was about to come inside the tent!

Pam's parents heard the girls scream. They came running outside to see what was wrong. "Be careful, Dad," Pam said. "There is a giant spider outside the tent!"

Pam heard her parents laugh and then watched them open the tent door. "Do you mean this?" her dad asked. He had a small tree branch in his hand. The branch had eight small leaves that looked like spider legs in the dark.

Everyone laughed at the girls' mistake. Pam and Kristy decided they were ready to go inside. Camping was fun, but they didn't want to see anything else that was scary!

Tarantulas

Tarantulas are a group of spiders that are hairy and large. They are found in warm climates. Some are found in warmer areas of the United States. Tarantulas can live for a long time. Tarantulas can live to be more than twenty years old.

The bird spider is a type of tarantula. It is one of the world's largest spiders. It is such a large spider that it can even eat a small bird!

Many people think that all tarantulas are harmful to humans. This is not true. The tarantulas that live in the United States have a bite that is like the sting of a bee. Some tarantulas do have a bite that is poisonous. One type of tarantula that lives in Australia has a bite that is very dangerous. Its poison is worse than a black widow spider.

The tarantula will always make some people afraid. Its large size and hairy body make it scary to some people. Knowing that most tarantulas cannot hurt someone helps people to not be afraid of this amazing spider.

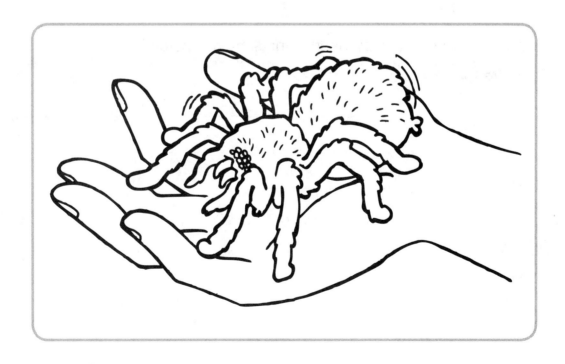

UNIT 19 QUESTIONS

Name   **Date**

The following pages have questions based on the texts from Unit 19. You may look at the stories to help answer any questions. Use the back of the page if you need extra space for writing your answers.

1 What are Pam and Kristy planning to do at the beginning of the story?

    (a) They are going to go to the circus.

    (b) They are going to Kristy's house.

    (c) They are going to go to the mall.

    (d) They are going to camp outside.

2 What is the same in both stories?

    (a) They both talk about camping in a tent.

    (b) They both talk about spiders.

    (c) They both talk about tarantulas.

    (d) They both talk about how to put up a tent.

3 Which sentence is NOT true about tarantulas?

    (a) Tarantulas like cold weather.

    (b) One type of tarantula eats birds.

    (c) Tarantulas can be found in the United States.

    (d) The bite of some tarantulas feels like a bee sting.

4 What does the word *climates* mean in the sentence below?

They are found in warm climates.

_____

_____

_____

5 Which word means the same as the word *large*?

    (a) tiny

    (b) huge

    (c) many

    (d) round

6 Do you think Pam and Kristy will ever camp outside again? Circle your answer.
Then explain your answer.

Yes / No because _____

_____.

7 Circle the picture that is most likely the tarantula. Then, explain why you chose
that picture.

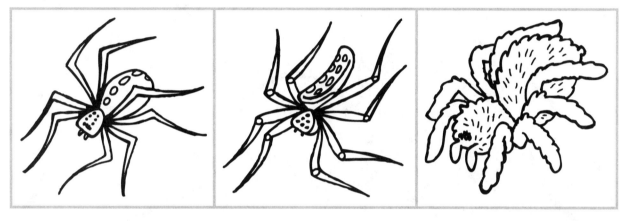

_____

_____

8 How do you know Pam cares about what happens to her father?

_____

_____

9 Use what you read and write a sentence that is true about tarantulas.

_____

_____

10 Think of three words or groups of words that would best describe a tarantula.
Write your answers on the lines.

a. _____

b. _____

c. _____

UNIT 19 | Name | Date

Time to Write!

Complete the graphic organizer about spiders. Research a type of spider. Write the name of the spider in the center space. Write facts about the spider on each of its legs.

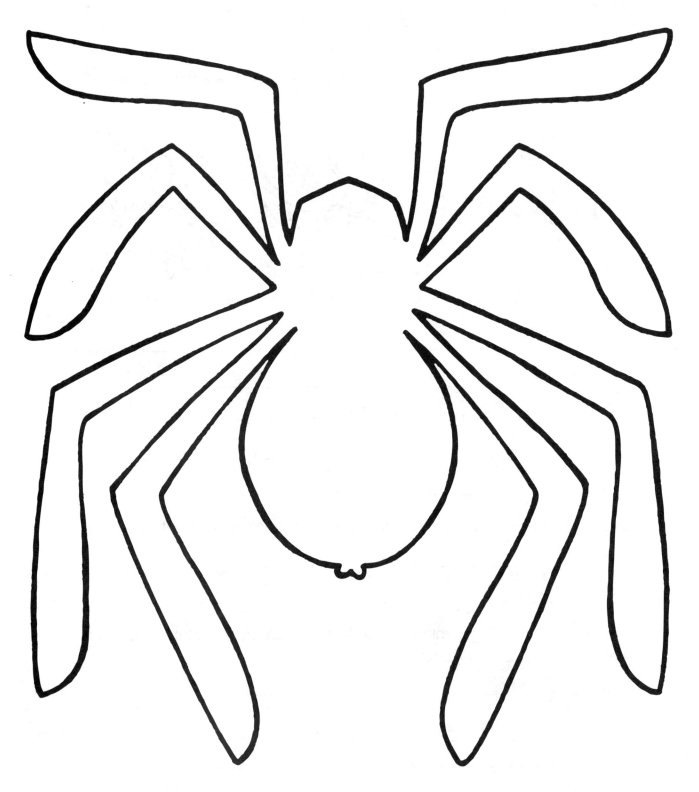

The Bravest of All

Tom was a knight. He fought for the king. He was one of the king's best knights. He was never afraid. He would do whatever needed to be done to protect the castle and to keep the king safe.

One day, the king called for Tom to go see him. When Tom saw the king, he knew something was wrong. The king began to tell Tom that a terrible dragon would not leave the kingdom alone. The dragon used its fire to destroy the villages. The dragon had to be stopped. The king trusted only Tom to help save the kingdom.

Tom knew what he had to do. He grabbed his sword. Then he got on his horse. He rode toward the place where the dragon had last been seen. It did not take long for Tom to find the dragon.

The dragon was ready for Tom. It began to fight. It breathed fire at Tom. It even tried to trap Tom with its sharp claws. But each time the dragon made a move, Tom was able to get away. The two fought back and forth with each other. Then, suddenly, there was a mighty roar. Tom was able to make a splendid move with his sword. He drove the tip into the belly of the great beast. The dragon was no more. Tom was truly the bravest of all the knights.

The next morning, Tom woke up in his own bed. He was not a knight any longer. He was just Tom. He grabbed his wooden sword from off the floor. He grabbed his wooden shield from underneath the bed. It had been a wonderful dream to fight a dragon and win. He swung his wooden sword at the boy reflected in the mirror. One day, he just knew he would be able to show everyone that he truly was a great knight and not just in his dreams!

Dragons

Dragons have been written about in stories for centuries. The dragon is not a real animal. In some stories, the dragon is a hero. In other stories, the dragon is evil.

Both good and evil dragons are usually described as large, lizard-like creatures that can breathe fire. These same dragons are also described as having long, scaly tails. Dragons were also said to have wings. They could fly through the sky, so it was hard for men to catch them.

In many of the old stories, dragons guarded great treasures. The treasures were hidden in the places where the dragons lived. Usually, the dragon lived in a cave inside a mountain. This made it even harder for someone to take the dragon's treasure.

Today, the image of a dragon can be seen in many places. There are cartoons with dragons. Dragons are characters in television shows and movies. In China, people wear dragon costumes during parades as a sign of good luck for the new year. People no longer believe dragons are living in faraway lands, but it is still interesting to imagine what it would have been like if dragons had really lived.

UNIT 20 QUESTIONS

Name

Date

The following pages have questions based on the texts from Unit 20. You may look at the stories to help answer any questions. Use the back of the page if you need extra space for writing your answers.

1 What do both stories have in common?

(a) Both stories tell about knights.

(b) Both stories tell about castles.

(c) Both stories tell about dragons.

(d) Both stories tell about dreams.

2 From the stories, you can tell that dragons are . . .

(a) no longer living.

(b) make-believe animals.

(c) still a problem for people.

(d) the largest animals to have ever lived on Earth.

3 What does the word *image* mean in the sentence below?

Today, the image of a dragon can be seen in many places.

(a) something that looks like something else

(b) something that sounds like something else

(c) something that does not look like something else

(d) something that is scary or mean

4 Which word best describes how Tom felt about his dream?

(a) scared

(b) wonderful

(c) afraid

(d) surprised

5 Write the sentence from the story that helped you to answer #4.

_____

_____

_____

6 Write two more sentences that tell something that could have happened in Tom's dream.

a. _____

_____

b. _____

_____

7 Write one fact that is true about dragons.

_____

_____

_____

8 From the story, what is something you can tell about the dragon Tom is fighting?

_____

_____

_____

9 Write two words that would best describe Tom when he was a knight.

a. _____

b. _____

10 What would be another good title for the story "The Bravest of All"?

_____

Explain why you think this is a good title for the story.

_____

_____

Time to Write!

Look at this picture of a shield.

A shield was used by a knight to help him in battle. The pictures on the shield all had special meaning to the knight.

For example, in the shield on the right, the picture of the heart might mean the knight's love for his family or for the king and his kingdom. The shields were also used so other people in battle would know who the knights were, so they did not accidentally hurt their friends.

Draw pictures in each of the spaces below to make your own shield. Explain what each picture means to you. Label each picture with a number from 1 to 4.

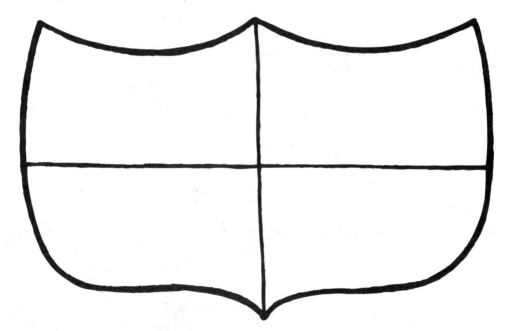

1. This picture means _____.

2. This picture means _____.

3. This picture means _____.

4. This picture means _____.

Something Extra: On the back of the page, draw a shield with four pictures for your school. Be sure to explain what each picture means.

A Family Feast

The turkey was almost done. Zoe could not wait to eat. Thanksgiving was her favorite holiday. She loved it the most because her grandparents always came. They lived far away from Zoe and her parents. They lived in another country. They always flew in to visit on Thanksgiving.

Zoe's grandparents were already seated at the table. Zoe's mother was letting her help get the food ready. It was the first time Zoe had been allowed to help with the cooking. They were using one of her grandmother's recipes. She hoped her grandmother would be surprised. Her grandmother did not know they were making one of her own special dishes.

Zoe's mother put the turkey on the table. Everyone thought it looked perfect. Zoe brought in the green beans. Then she got the rolls and put them in a basket. She put those on the table beside the beans.

"Is it time to eat?" Zoe's grandfather asked. "Everything looks perfect."

"Almost," Zoe's mother said. She winked at Zoe. Zoe disappeared into the kitchen again. When she came out, she had the sweet potatoes she had made using her grandmother's recipe. Her grandmother saw what she had done. She smiled as Zoe put the dish on the table right beside her.

"Now we can eat," Zoe said.

"I cannot wait to try this wonderful food," her grandmother said. She hugged Zoe tight.

Zoe knew this was a Thanksgiving she would never forget.

110

Giving Thanks

Thanksgiving is a special holiday. On this day, people remember to be thankful for what they have. The holiday is celebrated each year in November. Thanksgiving is usually a family holiday. Families get together and share many of their favorite foods and stories.

The holiday began long ago. The Pilgrims were the first to celebrate Thanksgiving with a feast. In 1621, the Pilgrims had a large crop and plenty of food. They had seen many days where there was not enough food. They were thankful for the good crop. They were thankful for the help given to them by the Natives. They had a feast that lasted for three days. They ate outdoors at large tables. Everyone enjoyed the wonderful foods.

President Abraham Lincoln made Thanksgiving Day a holiday for America. He listened to the idea of others and thought the country should have a day each year to celebrate. He thought a day of thanks was a good idea.

People today celebrate the holiday in many different ways. Some gather with their families. Others use the day to help those in need. Some spend time with friends. Thanksgiving will always be special for anyone who chooses to celebrate the day.

The following pages have questions based on the texts from Unit 21. You may look at the stories to help answer any questions. Use the back of the page if you need extra space for writing your answers.

1 When Zoe makes her grandmother's special dish, she is continuing a family tradition. What is a *tradition*?

    (a) something special that is passed down from one person in a family to another person

    (b) something that is done each week

    (c) something people want to forget

    (d) something that no one knows about

2 Who made Thanksgiving a national holiday?

    (a) Zoe

    (b) Zoe's grandmother

    (c) Abraham Lincoln

    (d) the Pilgrims

3 Why were the Pilgrims celebrating?

    (a) They had a good crop and plenty of food.

    (b) They were glad to be friends with the Natives.

    (c) They wanted to cook a lot of food.

    (d) They were leaving America.

4 What is a holiday that you celebrate? _____

Explain why you celebrate this day.

_____

_____

5 Which word best describes how Zoe's grandmother felt when she saw what Zoe had done?

    (a) proud

    (b) bored

    (c) sad

    (d) worried

6 Compare and contrast Thanksgiving to another holiday. Write the name of the holiday on the line. Write one way they are the same. Write one way they are different. (It does not have to be a holiday you celebrate.)

Thanksgiving and _____	Same	Different

7 Answer each question using what you know from the texts.

   a. Whose recipe does Zoe use for Thanksgiving dinner?

_____

   b. Why were Zoe's grandparents at her house?

_____

   c. Why were the Pilgrims thankful?

_____

8 What most likely happened after Zoe sat down with her family?

_____

9 Which word means nearly the same as *celebrate*?

  a hope   **b** party   **c** fight   **d** sleep

10 Think of another holiday you would like to know more about. Research the holiday. List two facts you learn.

   Holiday: _____

   1. _____

      _____

   2. _____

      _____

Time to Write!

All holidays were created by someone. Now it's your turn to make up your own holiday!
Answer each question to tell all about your new and special day.

Name of your holiday: _____

When is your holiday? _____

Why are you celebrating this special day? _____

_____

_____

What do people do on your holiday?_____

_____

_____

Does your holiday have any presents? *Yes / No* (Circle your answer.)

If yes, who gets the presents and why?

_____

_____

_____

Do adults or children like your holiday the best? Explain your answer.

_____

_____

_____

_____

Something Extra: On the back of the page, draw and color a picture of you celebrating
your new holiday.

Don't Rock the Boat

Meg loved going to her summer camp each year. For two weeks, she could play and swim and do lots of fun things with all of her friends. Her favorite thing about camp was riding in a canoe.

Last year, Meg had learned to canoe. At first, she did not know how to use a paddle. When she tried to paddle the boat, the boat would go in a circle. She could not make the canoe go straight. Then her teacher showed her how to use the oar. She had to paddle on one side of the boat. Then she had to paddle on the other side of the boat. Now she could make the canoe go anywhere she wanted it to go.

Meg was a good swimmer, but she always wore her lifejacket in the canoe. At the start of camp, she ran into a log hidden under the water. The log flipped her canoe. Meg and her friend ended up in the water. She had been so glad she had on her lifejacket. It did not take long for the others to help them, but it felt as though they were in the water for a long time because the water was cold.

When Meg got older, she wanted to go back to camp. She wanted to help the younger girls like some of the older girls did now. She could not wait to be the person who taught others how to canoe. She knew camp would always be a special part of her life.

Out on the Open Waters

Boats have always been important to people. People used boats to explore other lands. Boats are still used by people to visit places. They help people get food. They are even used to move goods from one place to another. There are many different types of boats. Some are used for work. Others are used for fun.

Large sailing ships were used to explore new worlds. Christopher Columbus and his men used ships with sails to explore. The three most famous ships sailed by Columbus were the *Niña*, the *Pinta*, and the *Santa María*. The largest of his three ships was the *Santa María*. Sailing ships were also used to ship goods from place to place. Tea came from China, and sugar came from the West Indies. Sailors brought things back from other parts of the world for everyone to enjoy.

People use boats today for all kinds of reasons. People use boats for fishing. Barges move goods up and down rivers. People enjoy riding in canoes and kayaks and spending time out on the water. It is hard to imagine a time when people won't enjoy spending time on boats and out on the water.

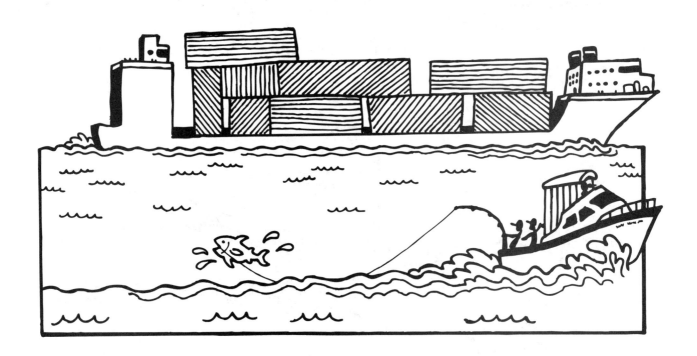

UNIT 22 QUESTIONS

Name

Date

The following pages have questions based on the texts from Unit 22. You may look at the stories to help answer any questions. Use the back of the page if you need extra space for writing your answers.

1 What is Meg's favorite thing to do at camp?

    (a) go swimming

    (b) go horseback riding

    (c) go hiking

    (d) go canoeing

2 What is one thing people do NOT use boats for?

    (a) catching fish

    (b) going on trips

    (c) exploring places

    (d) hiking in the woods

3 What type of boat or ship did Columbus use during his trips at sea?

    (a) a ship with sails

    (b) a boat with oars

    (c) a boat with a motor

    (d) a canoe with paddles

4 Write the sentence from the story "Out on the Open Waters" that helped you to answer #3.

_____

_____

_____

_____

5 What is the same about the two stories?

    (a) They both talk about shipwrecks.

    (b) They both talk about some type of boat.

    (c) They both talk about ships with sails.

    (d) They both talk about Christopher Columbus.

6 Answer the questions about the story "Don't Rock the Boat."

  a. What part of canoeing did Meg first have trouble doing?

  _____

  _____

  b. What happened to Meg's canoe when she hit a log?

  _____

  _____

  c. Why does Meg want to go back to camp when she is older?

  _____

  _____

7 What is one way a sailing ship is like a canoe?

  _____

  _____

8 What is one way a sailing ship is different from a canoe?

  _____

  _____

9 Why does Meg always wear her lifejacket when she is canoeing?

  _____

  _____

10 From the story, list one item sailors would bring from other parts of the world.

  _____

  Why do you think this item had to be shipped from one place to another place?

  _____

  _____

11 Imagine you were an explorer and you found a new world. Write what you would say as you stepped off the ship and onto the land.

  _____

  _____

Time to Write!

Imagine you are the captain of a ship. You and your crew cannot find any land. You have been at sea for over twenty days. Complete the captain's log and write about what life at sea is like for you and your crew.

CAPTAIN'S LOG

DAY 20: _____

_____

_____

_____

_____

DAY 21: _____

_____

_____

_____

_____

_____

DAY 22: WE HAVE SPOTTED LAND! _____

_____

_____

_____

_____

Taking a Closer Look

Mrs. Smith told everyone to be careful. The class was lining up to use a microscope. Gabe had never looked into a microscope before. He could not wait to see what things would look like through the scope. Mrs. Smith told the class everyone would get a turn. She only had one microscope for them to look at, but Gabe knew Mrs. Smith would keep her word. She always did what she said she was going to do.

Finally, it was Gabe's turn. He put his eye next to the special piece where he needed to look. Under the scope was a slide Mrs. Smith had put for each student to see. The slide had a flower inside. Gabe could see all the parts of the flower. He was amazed by how well he could see each part.

Gabe did not want to stop looking, but he knew it was time for another student to have a turn. All of the students seemed to be as excited as Gabe was. They were all talking about everything that they could see with the microscope.

When it was time to leave the lab, Gabe hated to go. Mrs. Smith promised the class they would come back tomorrow. She told them she would have something else special for them to look at tomorrow. Gabe could not wait. As they walked back to class, he wondered what it would be like to be a scientist. He thought it would be great to discover new things and to get to use a microscope every day. Gabe wondered how many of the other students wanted to be scientists now, too. Just look at what Mrs. Smith had started with her wonderful lesson!

Microscopes

In 1590, a man named Hans Janssen and his son made a wonderful discovery. They were working in their lab. They put one glass lens on top of another one. They looked at an object under the lenses. They could see it more clearly. This was the start of the microscope.

With a microscope, a person can see an object more clearly and close up. Once it was invented, people could also see things that had never been seen before. Cells, bacteria, and viruses were now all things that could be seen. People did not know about these things they had never seen!

Because people now knew about such small organisms, certain illnesses could be cured. The scientist, Louis Pasteur, was able to use a microscope to help him understand what caused many diseases. Once people knew what caused a disease, they were often able to find a way to stop or treat an illness.

Today, people use microscopes every day. Scientists still use them to help make important discoveries. Doctors in hospitals use them. Even students use microscopes. Microscopes help everyone to take a closer look at the amazing things in our world!

The following pages have questions based on the texts from Unit 23. You may look at the stories to help answer any questions. Use the back of the page if you need extra space for writing your answers.

1 Why has Mrs. Smith taken the class to the lab?

(a) They are going to look through a telescope.

(b) They are going to do an experiment.

(c) They are going to do some homework.

(d) They are going to look through a microscope.

2 Which sentence is NOT true about microscopes?

(a) People can see objects better using a microscope.

(b) Only scientists can look at objects through microscopes.

(c) People have been able to cure diseases with the help of microscopes.

(d) People discovered cells by looking through a microscope.

3 What do the two stories have in common?

(a) They both talk about great scientists.

(b) They both talk about microscopes.

(c) They both talk about the invention of the microscope.

(d) The two stories have nothing in common.

4 Which story best tells how the microscope was invented?

_____

5 What happens to Gabe after he looks through the microscope?

(a) He wants to be a scientist when he grows up.

(b) He starts to feel sick.

(c) He does not want to come back to the lab.

(d) He gets pushed into the microscope, and it breaks.

6 List in order what happens to Gabe at school. Use the numbers 1 to 4. Put 1 by what happened first. Put 4 by what happened last.

_____ Gabe sees a flower.

_____ Gabe thinks he might want to be a scientist.

_____ Mrs. Smith takes her class into the lab.

_____ Gabe waits for his turn to look using the microscope.

7 Which word best describes how Gabe would feel the next time the class gets to look through the microscope?

(a) scared   (c) nervous

(b) excited   (d) anxious

8 Explain one way people use microscopes today.

_____

_____

_____

9 Write two sentences telling what the story "Taking a Closer Look" is about.

_____

_____

_____

10 Which picture would go best with the story "Taking a Closer Look"? Circle it. Then tell why you chose the picture you did.

_____

Time to Write!

The microscope was a great invention. Look up information about another invention.
Use the space below to tell what you find out.

Name of the invention: _____

Name of the inventor: _____

What does the invention do? _____

_____

_____

How has it helped people? _____

_____

_____

Is the invention still being used today? *Yes / No* (Circle one.)

Explain why or why not: _____

_____

_____

Would you ever use this invention? *Yes / No* (Circle one.)

Why or why not? _____

_____

_____

Something Extra: On the back of the page, draw and color a picture of the invention.

A Night to Remember

Misty sat in front of the television. Her mother told her that tonight she would get to watch the Olympic Winter Games. The Games were sporting events between people from different countries. The people try to win medals for their countries. Her mother told her the Games only happen every four years. She told her there were winter and summer games.

Misty did not remember the last Winter Olympic Games. She had been only four years old the first time she watched them. She was too young to remember. Her mother told her she loved watching the people skate on the ice. Tonight, she was going to watch the skaters. She hoped she still liked it.

It was finally time for the show to begin. First, there were people who were riding snowboards. Then, Misty saw people skiing. Finally, it was time for the skaters. Misty was glued to the television as the first skater went out onto the ice.

The music became louder as the skater began her dance. She flew across the ice. She jumped and twirled. She landed each time perfectly. Misty could not sit still. She cheered on the skater, hoping she would win a medal. Her skating was one of the most amazing things Misty had ever seen.

When it was time to go to bed, Misty could not stop thinking about the Olympic Games. She told her mother she wanted to learn to skate just like an Olympian. Her mother told her it would take years of practice to be as good as they were. She told Misty they would go tomorrow and sign her up for skating lessons.

Misty was so happy. She knew she would never forget tonight. When people would ask her why she wanted to learn to skate, she knew she would always know just what to tell them.

The History of the Olympic Games

The Olympic Games happen every two years. There are winter and summer games. The athletes in the Games spend the time in between training for the next Olympic Games. The Games involve people from all over the world. Each person tries to win a medal for his or her country. At the Olympic Games, a gold medal is the highest prize a person can win. People playing in the Games can also win silver and bronze medals.

The Olympic Games began in Greece many years ago. The first known Games were played in 776 B.C. The first Olympic Games only had one game. The game was a race. There are still races in today's Games. Other sports were later added to the Games.

In the beginning, women were not able to play in any of the Games. Only men and boys could be Olympians. Anyone who won a game was given a crown made of olive leaves. He was treated as a hero.

Today's Olympic Games are only a little like the Games of long ago. There are still heroes, and the winners are still very special. People who are in the games today are on television. They make money by helping companies sell products. For example, an excellent skier might help advertise a type of winter gloves. Many Olympic winners become famous. They may or may not play again in other Olympic Games. No matter what the athletes decide to do, the people watching the Olympic Games are always proud when someone from their country wins a medal.

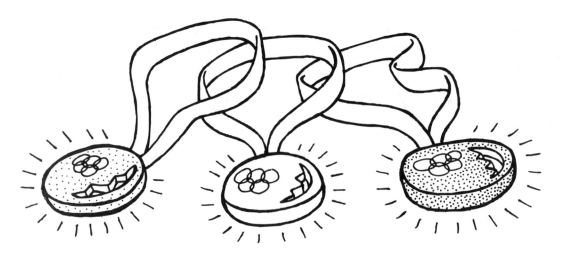

The following pages have questions based on the texts from Unit 24. You may look at the stories to help answer any questions. Use the back of the page if you need extra space for writing your answers.

1 In paragraph 3 of "A Night to Remember," what does it mean when it says "Misty was glued to the television"?

    (a) Misty had glue on her clothes.

    (b) Misty was not going to move.

    (c) Misty was not going to watch.

    (d) Misty could not move.

2 What is the same about the two stories?

    (a) They both talk about ice skating.

    (b) They both talk about the history of the Olympic Games.

    (c) They both talk about the Olympic Games.

    (d) They both talk about the first Olympic Games.

3 Why is the story most likely called "A Night to Remember"?

_____

_____

_____

4 What was the first Olympic game?

    (a) racing

    (b) ice skating

    (c) swimming

    (d) dancing

5 What is one way today's Olympic Games are the same as the first Olympic Games?

_____

_____

_____

6 What is one reason you think the Olympic Games do not happen every year?

_____

_____

7 Why did Misty not remember seeing the Olympic Games the first time she watched them?

_____

_____

8 Look at the three pictures. Circle the picture that might have happened in the first Olympic Games.

9 Which sentences from either of the stories helped you to answer #8?

_____

_____

_____

10 What is one thing that is NOT the same about the first Olympic Games and today's Olympic Games?

_____

_____

Time to Write!

Many Olympic heroes find their faces on the boxes of cereal. Their images are used to help sell the cereal.

In the space below, create your own box of cereal. Design the cover for the box. Be sure to draw the face of someone special on the box of cereal. The person does NOT have to be a real person. Add three facts about the cereal to include on your box.

The Best Book Ever

The teacher's voice was soft and clear. All of the children in her class were trying not to cry. The teacher was reading to the class the last chapter of the story *Charlotte's Web* by E.B. White. Riley loved all the characters in the book. Wilbur the pig and Charlotte the spider were two of her favorites.

As the teacher finished the book, Riley was sad. She did not want the book to end. She did not want any of the characters in the story to have anything bad happen to them. Still, she thought the book was one of the best she had ever heard. She could not wait to go home and tell her mother all about it.

When Riley got home, she told her mother about the book. She was surprised to find out her mother already knew the entire story.

"I read that book when I was your age," her mother told her. "I have never forgotten it."

Riley's mother went into her bedroom. She came back out to the kitchen where Riley was sitting. She held out an old copy of *Charlotte's Web*. She also had a copy of another book, *Stuart Little*.

"My mother gave me these books when I was a little girl. I want you to have them now."

Riley was happy to get the gifts from her mother. Then she had a great idea.

"Could we read these books together?" she asked her mother.

Riley's mother said yes. Riley noticed there were tears in her mother's eyes even though she was happy. Riley was sure she understood just how her mother felt.

A Wonderful Writer

E.B. White is the author of the children's books *Charlotte's Web* and *Stuart Little*. He was born in 1899. As a young boy, he had a large family. He grew up with parents who loved children. When he was older, he went to college. At first, he worked as a reporter. He wrote for a magazine called *The New Yorker*. He met his wife while working there.

Mr. White wrote lots of different articles for his job. He knew he wanted to do something else with his writing. So he began to write books for children. In 1945, he wrote a story that many children know and love. The story was about a small child who looked like a mouse. His name and the name of the book was *Stuart Little*. Now there are movies all about the famous mouse.

In 1952, he wrote the book *Charlotte's Web*. In this book, a spider named Charlotte tries to save her friend Wilbur the pig. The spider writes words in her web. The words tell how great Wilbur is. Everyone believes Wilbur is an amazing animal that lives thanks to Charlotte's help.

E.B. White's books have been read by millions of children. His words have brought smiles to the faces of so many people. It is hard to imagine a world where Stuart Little and Charlotte or Wilbur do not exist.

UNIT 25 QUESTIONS

Name _____ **Date** _____

The following pages have questions based on the texts from Unit 25. You may look at the stories to help answer any questions. Use the back of the page if you need extra space for writing your answers.

1 Why were the children trying not to cry when they heard the teacher read the story?

(a) The children didn't want anything bad to happen.

(b) The children did not feel well.

(c) The children did not like the story.

(d) The teacher was hurt.

2 Why has Riley's mother never forgotten the book?

(a) She did not like the book.

(b) She liked the book.

(c) She lost the book.

(d) She wanted to read a different book.

3 Now that Riley has the book *Stuart Little,* she will probably . . .

(a) enjoy the book.

(b) never read the book.

(c) forget she has the book.

(d) give the book to a friend.

4 Which sentence is NOT true about E.B. White?

(a) He only wrote one book.

(b) He wrote at least two children's books.

(c) He came from a large family.

(d) He wrote books for children.

5 What does Charlotte do to help save Wilbur?

_____

_____

_____

_____

6 What will Riley and her mother most likely do with the books Riley's mother gave her?

_____

_____

7 Are E.B. White's children's stories fiction or nonfiction? How do you know?

_____

_____

_____

8 What is one thing the two stories have in common?

_____

_____

_____

9 What is special about the books Riley's mother gives to Riley?

_____

_____

_____

10 Think of a book that is special to you. What is the title of the book?

_____

Give two reasons why the book is special to you.

a. _____

_____

b. _____

_____

Time to Write!

The setting for *Charlotte's Web* was on a farm. Think of a farm animal you want to know more about. Research the animal. Write at least five facts about the animal you choose.

Farm Animal: _____

Fact 1: _____

_____

_____

Fact 2: _____

_____

_____

Fact 3: _____

_____

_____

Fact 4: _____

_____

_____

Fact 5: _____

_____

_____

Pigs with a Purpose

Peter held his nose. The smell coming from the pond was not good. There were pigs everywhere. Some were wallowing in the mud. Some were walking around the edge of the pond. Some were using their noses to dig in the mud. He didn't know why his uncle wanted so many pigs by his pond. Peter knew he would never be able to fish at the pond. The smell was too strong to enjoy a day by the water with his fishing pole.

"Well, Peter," Uncle John said, "what do you think of the pigs?"

"The pigs are sort of cute, Uncle John, but they sure do smell bad. Why did you put all these pigs down near my favorite place to fish?"

Uncle John laughed at the face Peter made. His nose was all wrinkled up. Peter's voice even sounded funny. He was trying to talk without breathing through his nose. Peter could not understand why his uncle thought he was funny even if he wasn't trying to be silly.

"I know how much you like to fish, Peter, but your favorite fishing spot had a leak!"

"How can a pond have a leak?" Peter asked.

"Somewhere, the water was slowly leaking out of the pond. That meant all the fish were going to die. I needed a way to stop the leak, but the problem was I didn't know where the water was going out. It's not like a bathtub. In a tub, you know the water is going down the drain. I needed a way to stop the entire thing from leaking."

"So, that's what the pigs are for?"

"That's right, Peter. The pigs will move all of the dirt around until they stop the leak. Then we will move the pigs away from your pond. You will have your fishing spot back with no leaks!"

"All right, Uncle John, I've changed my mind," Peter said. "I like pigs with a purpose after all!"

Pigs for Pets?

Would you ever think about living in the same house with a pig? Some people would! Many people think potbellied pigs are the best pets to have. Potbellied pigs are sometimes adopted or bought by people to be indoor pets. These unusual swine can make good pets for many different reasons. They even have many traits that are the same as dogs. For example, they can be trained to do tricks. They can be walked on leashes. They can be housebroken. Also, they can be great company for the pet owner. Potbellied pigs are a lot of fun for someone who wants an unusual pet.

Having a potbellied pig for a pet can also have its share of problems. These pigs need a lot of food. They will spend much of their time trying to find something to eat. Anyone with a pig for a pet must be sure to keep an eye on where he or she puts his or her food, or the pig might find a tasty snack!

Potbellied pigs do not stay as small as some people think they do. In fact, they can grow to be rather big. Many times, people who get a baby potbellied pig for an indoor pet do not expect such a small animal to grow into such a large one. Sadly, because of their unexpected large size, many of these unique pets are abandoned by their owners. Just how big can these small pigs grow to be? Many adult potbellied pigs grow up to be about the same size as a large dog.

For many people, the potbellied pig makes a good pet because most breeds have very little hair. Also, pet pigs do not shed. Some people are allergic to cats and dogs. They love the idea of a pet that does not make them itch or sneeze. Another good thing about potbellied pigs is ticks and fleas do not like the tough skin of the pig.

Not everyone can have a pig for a pet. Pigs are considered to be livestock. Many places have rules that say people cannot have livestock as pets. No matter where someone lives, a person should really think about the decision before getting a potbellied pig as a pet.

UNIT 26 QUESTIONS

Name _____ **Date** _____

The following pages have questions based on the texts from Unit 26. You may look at the stories to help answer any questions. Use the back of the page if you need extra space for writing your answers.

1 Why does Uncle John need the pigs?

    (a) The pigs are his pets.

    (b) He is taking the pigs to the fair.

    (c) He bought the pigs as a surprise for Peter.

    (d) The pigs will stop the leak in the pond.

2 Write the sentence or sentences from the text that helped you answer #1.

_____

_____

_____

3 What does the word *wallowing* mean in this sentence?

Some were wallowing in the mud.

    (a) sleeping

    (b) rolling

    (c) strolling

    (d) hopping

4 List one reason why potbellied pigs might make good pets.

_____

_____

_____

5 After reading the texts, which statement can you say is true?

    (a) All pigs are pets.

    (b) All pigs live outside.

    (c) Pigs can be both pets and livestock.

    (d) Pigs should never be pets.

6 Which happens first in the story?

　　(a) Peter tells Uncle John he likes the pigs.

　　(b) Peter sees all the pigs at the pond.

　　(c) Peter's uncle explains the pigs are going to fix a leak in the pond.

　　(d) Peter asks his uncle why there are so many pigs.

7 What does Peter like to do at the pond?

　　(a) swim

　　(b) fish

　　(c) play

　　(d) walk

8 What do the texts "Pigs with a Purpose" and "Pigs for Pets?" have in common?

　　(a) They both talk about what pigs can do.

　　(b) They both take place on a farm.

　　(c) They both have the characters Peter and his uncle in them.

　　(d) They both say that pigs are better pets than dogs or cats.

9 Which sentence is an opinion?

　　(a) Many people think potbellied pigs are the best pets to have.

　　(b) Potbellied pigs are sometimes adopted or bought by people to be indoor pets.

　　(c) These pigs need a lot of food.

　　(d) Pigs are considered to be livestock.

10 Write two sentences from the text "Pigs for Pets?" that are facts.

_____

_____

_____

_____

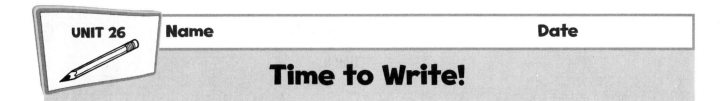

Time to Write!

Part 1

Some writers use webs to organize their ideas. Use the writer's web below to write down some facts about pigs.

Let your teacher help you look up some information about pigs if you don't already know much about these animals. Use what you learn to finish the web.

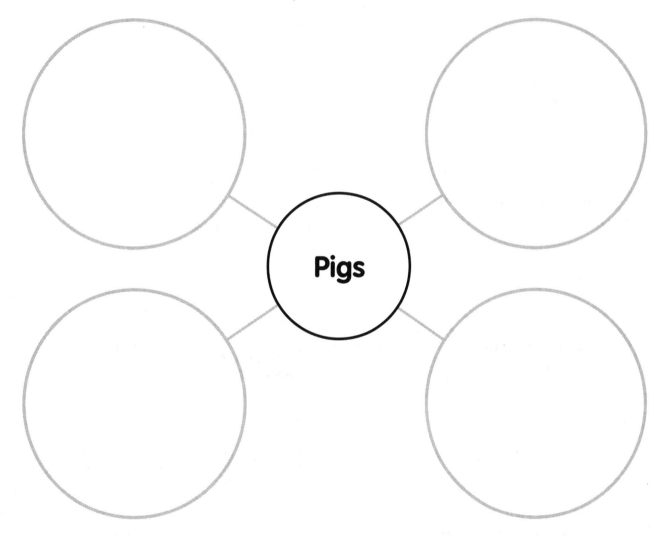

Pigs

Part 2

Now that you know a little bit more about pigs, write your own story with at least one pig as a character. You can use the back of the page or another piece of paper to write your story. You can also draw and color a picture to go with your writing.

Answer Key

Unit 1
1. d
2. a; He wanted a real pet, not a rock.
3. a and c
4. d
5. There is no such thing as a perfect pet. Also the "pet rock" was a joke, not a real pet.
6.–8. Answers will vary.
9. b
10. People thought the idea was funny.

Unit 2
1. a
2. b
3. Answers will vary.
4. d
5. b
6.–8. Answers will vary.
9. nonfiction passage
10. Answers will vary.

Unit 3
1. b
2. c
3. flying
4. b
5. c
6.–10. Answers will vary.

Unit 4
1. a and c
2. d
3. Answers will vary.
4. b
5. d
6. Answers will vary.
7. She saw a show on television.
8. Answers will vary.
9. d
10. Answers will vary.

Unit 5
1. b
2. The outside was made of stone.
3. a
4. c
5.–7. Answers will vary.
8. They would be the towers for the castle.
9. The cans would be the towers.
10. b
11. Answers will vary.

Unit 6
1. a and d
2. He sees one in a store.
3. He knows he already has two great pets, so he no longer wants the robot dog.
4. b
5. Answers will vary.
6. a
7.–8. Answers will vary.
9. People can't go to Mars, but robots can go and take pictures.
10. c

Unit 7
1. b
2. b
3. c
4. b
5. They scream and run.
6. Answers will vary.
7. a and c
8. It is a fact or real.
9.–10. Answers will vary.

Unit 8
1. a
2. b
3. Answers will vary.
4. a
5. c
6. People coming to America went through Ellis Island. (or) People coming to America did go through Ellis Island.
7. Answers will vary.
8. a
9. The Statue of Liberty
10. Answers will vary.

Unit 9
1. a
2. c
3. The text did not say anything about jellyfish staying on the bottom of the ocean. All of the other answers could be found in the story.
4. d
5. a
6. Other people need a turn to see them.
7. Answers will vary.
8. d
9. They use the tentacles to catch their food.
10. b

Answer Key *(cont.)*

Unit 10

1. b
2. a
3. d
4. Answers will vary about either New Year's Day or MLK, Jr. Day.
5. Answers will vary.
6. The word *all* should be circled.
7. Either of these two sentences can be used to help support the answer for #6:
   For some people, January is a very cold month.
   For other people, January is a very warm month.
8. The god Janus has two faces—one sees the past, and the other sees the future.
9. Mike lived where it was cold, and his grandmother wanted to share the beach with him.
10. Answers will vary.

Unit 11

1. a
2. The elephant is the largest land animal.
3. b
4. d
5. the area where an animal lives
6. They are big. They are a lot of fun.
7.–8. Answers will vary.
9. The elephants are large, but they are also animals that like to play.
10. Answers will vary.

Unit 12

1. a
2. c
3. b
4. There are several sentences in the stories that support the answer for #3.
5. c
6. Dan has been to Disney World "many times" so he may have ridden a rollercoaster before.
7. a
8.–10. Answers will vary.

Unit 13

1. d
2. a
3. c
4. d
5. People were scared.
6. Answers will vary.
7. They thought the play was real and that aliens had landed on Earth.
8. No. The parents in the audience were using modern technology to take pictures. The radio play happened before there was television, computers, etc.
9.–10. Answers will vary.

Unit 14

1. c
2. d
3. Answers will vary.
4. b
5. d
6. They made a strange noise.
7. Conner and Emma
8. c
9. The Wright brothers used the box kite to help them design their airplanes.
10. Yes; answers will vary.

Unit 15

1. a
2. b
3. Beatrix Potter first began writing for a little boy she knew who was sick.
4. a
5. b
6. Answers will vary.
7. She thinks something has happened to her rabbits.
8. They both talk about rabbits that are important to different people.
9. b
10. She would like them. She likes rabbits, and the main character is a rabbit.

Unit 16

1. a
2. b
3. b
4. b
5.–8. Answers will vary.
9. d
10. Answers will vary.

Unit 17

1. b
2. b
3. b
4. b
5. If you are lucky, the only teeth you will lose are the baby ones!
6. Answers will vary.
7. a
8.–9. Answers will vary.
10. a

Answer Key *(cont.)*

Unit 18
1. b
2. a
3. a
4. a
5. She thinks it might be broken.
6. Students should circle the ribcage; answers will vary.
7. 1, 4, 3, 2
8. Mitch loves to ride his bike.
9. Answers will vary.
10. a

Unit 19
1. d
2. b
3. a
4. the areas where they live
5. b
6. Answers will vary.
7. Students should circle the third picture; answers will vary.
8. She says, "Be careful, Dad."
9.–10. Answers will vary.

Unit 20
1. c
2. b
3. a
4. b
5. It had been a wonderful dream to fight a dragon and win.
6.–10. Answers will vary.

Unit 21
1. a
2. c
3. a
4. Answers will vary.
5. a
6. Answers will vary.
7. a. her grandmother's recipe
   b. visiting for the holiday
   c. good crop and plenty of food
8. Answers will vary.
9. b
10. Answers will vary.

Unit 22
1. d
2. d
3. a
4. Christopher Columbus and his men used ships with sails to explore.
5. b
6. a. using the oars/paddles
   b. It tipped over.
   c. She wants to help others at the camp.
7.–8. Answers will vary.
9. The lifejacket helped her when her canoe flipped.
10. tea or sugar; answers will vary
11. Answers will vary.

Unit 23
1. d
2. b
3. b
4. Microscopes
5. a
6. 3, 4, 1, 2
7. b
8.–9. Answers will vary.
10. Students should circle the picture of the boy looking through the microscope; answers will vary.

Unit 24
1. b
2. c
3. Answers will vary.
4. a
5.–6. Answers will vary.
7. She was too young to remember.
8. Students should circle the picture of the person running.
9. Answers will vary but should include something about the only event in the first Olympic Games was a race.
10. Answers will vary.

Unit 25
1. a
2. b
3. a
4. a
5. She writes words about him in her web to convince people he is an amazing pig.
6. They will read the books together.
7. fiction—The mouse is like a little boy; animals do not talk in real life.
8. Answers will vary.
9. They were given to her by her mother.
10. Answers will vary.

Unit 26
1. d
2. The pigs will move all of the dirt around until they stop the leak.
3. b
4. Answers will vary.
5. c
6. b
7. b
8. a
9. a
10. Answers will vary.

Meeting Standards

Each passage and activity meets one or more of the following Common Core State Standards ©
Copyright 2010. National Governors Association Center for Best Practices and Council of Chief State
School Officers. All rights reserved. For more information about the Common Core State Standards, go
to *http://www.corestandards.org/* or *http://www.teachercreated.com/standards/*.

Reading: Literature	Passages and Activities
Key Ideas and Details	
ELA.RL.2.1: Ask and answer such questions as *who, what, where, when, why,* and *how* to demonstrate understanding of key details in a text.	All fiction
ELA.RL.2.3: Describe how characters in a story respond to major events and challenges.	Unit 1, Unit 8, Unit 10, Unit 15, Unit 18
Craft and Structure	
ELA.RL.2.5: Describe the overall structure of a story, including describing how the beginning introduces the story and the ending concludes the action.	Unit 3
Integration of Knowledge and Ideas	
ELA.RL.2.7: Use information gained from the illustrations and words in a print or digital text to demonstrate understanding of its characters, setting, or plot.	All fiction
Range of Reading and Level of Text Complexity	
ELA.RL.2.10: By the end of the year, read and comprehend literature, including stories and poetry, in the grades 2–3 text complexity band proficiently, with scaffolding as needed at the high end of the range.	All fiction
Reading: Informational Text	**Passages and Activities**
Key Ideas and Details	
ELA.RI.2.1: Ask and answer such questions as *who, what, where, when, why,* and *how* to demonstrate understanding of key details in a text.	All nonfiction
ELA.RI.2.2: Identify the main topic of a multiparagraph text as well as the focus of specific paragraphs within the text.	Unit 7

Meeting Standards *(cont.)*

Craft and Structure	
ELA.RI.2.4: Determine the meaning of words and phrases in a text relevant to a *grade 2 topic or subject area*.	Unit 3, Unit 4, Unit 7, Unit 8, Unit 10, Unit 11, Unit 19, Unit 21
Integration of Knowledge and Ideas	
ELA.RI.2.7: Explain how specific images (e.g., a diagram showing how a machine works) contribute to and clarify a text.	Unit 18, Unit 19, Unit 23
ELA.RI.2.9: Compare and contrast the most important points presented by two texts on the same topic.	All units
Range of Reading and Level of Text Complexity	
ELA.RI.2.10: By the end of year, read and comprehend informational texts, including history/social studies, science, and technical texts, in the grades 2–3 text complexity band proficiently, with scaffolding as needed at the high end of the range.	All nonfiction
Writing	**Passages and Activities**
Text Types and Purposes	
ELA.W.2.2: Write informative/explanatory texts in which they introduce a topic, use facts and definitions to develop points, and provide a concluding statement or section.	Unit 1, Unit 6, Unit 21
ELA.W.2.3: Write narratives in which they recount a well-elaborated event or short sequence of events, include details to describe actions, thoughts, and feelings, use temporal words to signal event order, and provide a sense of closure.	Unit 3, Unit 4, Unit 5, Unit 7, Unit 8, Unit 9, Unit 13, Unit 15, Unit 16, Unit 22
Research to Build and Present Knowledge	
ELA.W.2.7: Participate in shared research and writing projects (e.g., read a number of books on a single topic to produce a report; record science observations).	Unit 23, Unit 25, Unit 26
ELA.W.2.8: Recall information from experiences or gather information from provided sources to answer a question.	Unit 10, Unit 18